Raised-Bed Vegetable Gardening Made Simple

The Three-Module Home Vegetable Garden

RAYMOND NONES

The Countryman Press
Woodstock, Vermont

RAISED-BED VEGETABLE GARDENING MADE SIMPLE
The Three-Module Home Vegetable Garden

Please read this: The author and the publisher have done their best to
give useful and accurate information. But be aware that there are many
variables in gardening and many facts are subject to differing interpre-
tations. All of the recommendations are made without guarantee. You
have the final responsibility to check all material you read here as to
suitability, or accuracy, before relying on it. Of necessity the author and
the publisher disclaim any liability in connection with the use of the
information in this book.

Published by The Countryman Press
Woodstock, VT 05091
Visit our Web site at www.countrymanpress.com

ISBN 978-0-88150-896-3

Mixed Sources
Product group from well-managed
forests, controlled sources and
recycled wood or fiber
www.fsc.org   Cert no. SCS-COC-002464
©1996 Forest Stewardship Council

Printed in the United States by Versa Press, Peoria, Illinois.

10 9 8 7 6 5 4 3

This book is dedicated to the memory of my father, the late Gian B. Nones

Preface

I was born and raised in a small village amid the hills and hollows of western Pennsylvania. Back then times were hard, jobs were few, money was scarce, and everyone bought their groceries on credit from Tomlinson's, the only store in the community.

What were plentiful were vegetable gardens. One could be found in practically every backyard. They provided a vital portion of a family's food.

As did my father's: He loved gardening, and every season as he worked the garden my brothers and I were there with him, doing what had to be done. And there was plenty that had to be done: spading, cultivating, unending trips down to the creek refilling the watering can, and every evening, if there was any possibility of frost, placing a tin can over the newly planted tomato and pepper plants.

Then, little by little, as the plants grew, the grocery bills shrank. Tomatoes were eaten out of hand as snacks, lettuce was plucked just minutes before the salad was served, and corn was picked only when the water in the pot began to boil.

When, after many years' remove, I had the opportunity to start a vegetable garden of my own, those memories were my motivation.

This book attempts to reflect the purpose of all of those hard-times backyard gardens. That is: vegetable gardening, although it can be a source of great enjoyment, is in essence a serious matter, *an important food source.*

During World War II, for health and economic reasons, Americans were encouraged to establish what were called Victory Gardens to grow their own vegetables.

The public responded, and it was estimated that those little gardens produced a remarkable 30 to 40 percent of the country's food supply during that period.

That was a long time ago, but the rationale for such gardens is timeless, and your backyard vegetable garden today can still contribute not only to your well-being but to the nation's as well.

Introduction

Any piece of land that is growing weeds or grass can just as well be growing vegetables. There are only two requirements, the area (or areas) where the plants are to be grown must: 1) receive at least 6 to 8 hours of sunshine a day, and 2) be free of tree roots. If you have a plot that meets those conditions, you can enjoy the benefit of having a supply of vegetables right in your own backyard, freeing you from being solely dependent on the supermarket. Homegrown vegetables cost less, are fresher, and taste better than store bought. Also, if organically grown, which is the method described in this book, they will not have been exposed to harmful chemical fertilizers and toxic pesticides.

Vegetables go a long way to keeping you healthy as they are one of the very best sources of important vitamins and minerals. Plus, beyond your physical well-being, gardening will also keep you mentally healthy. Working outdoors, close to nature, growing living things, gives a unique satisfaction.

Anyone with a parcel of land, regardless of size, should strongly consider devoting at least a part of it to vegetable gardening. The physical, economic, and psychological rewards that can be derived from this activity are just too compelling not to give it a try.

Gardens come in all shapes and sizes: How big or how small will depend on many factors. The three-module home vegetable garden was specifically developed to meet the needs of the average family and will fit into the average-size backyard. It can be maintained by one person and, since it is intensively cropped, can be more productive than a much larger plot. It is also versatile; if a larger garden is wanted, additional modules can be added at any time without limit.

Once the area to be planted is selected, the next decision to be made is what to grow. In this book specific crops have been recommended. The types and varieties have been carefully selected for a wide range of reasons. They are proven performers which provide a continuous harvest from spring up into late fall. Even so, it is recognized that preferences vary and there may be vegetables included that are not liked. Since one of the reasons for having a garden is to grow what you want and use, feel free to substitute, tailor the crops grown to your taste and needs.

That aside, for first time gardeners, it is suggested that they plant the selected vegetables to start. Once they have gone through the first season they will be in a better position to know what changes, if any, need to be made to suit their particular situation. The one plant that practically everyone considers an absolute must is the tomato. It is such an important fruit and is so productive that one shouldn't even think about replacing it.

Whether you are an experienced gardener or a novice, it is suggested that you read the entire book all the way through so that you understand the modular system before doing any actual work. Then it can be referred to at every step, as necessary, throughout the season.

In addition to the personal benefits derived from growing your own crops, on another level, your garden will help in alleviating the food shortage that exists in many parts of the world. You may think that your little plot will not make much of a difference, but when multiplied by many, many similar backyard patches it all adds up to having a major impact. The commercially produced food that would have been consumed by home gardeners is now available to the hungry.

By the same token, a similar "ripple effect" would be had if organic methods were used by all of those who are engaged in growing vegetables. Recycling is a major factor in waste management operations. Using composting techniques, kitchen scraps and fall leaves become a resource instead of a disposal problem. And the world's environment is better for it.

1

Searching for a better way

Growing up, I was taught the conventional method of gardening. It is a good method with a proven track record. But when I started my own garden I began to question everything that I had been taught. No gardening procedure was accepted as the "correct way," it was only accepted as "one way." Was there a better way? One could find out only by looking for alternatives.

To seek answers I began researching all aspects of what is involved in the growing of plants. Besides studying advanced fundamentals, I was particularly interested in learning more about some of the unconventional systems that were being practiced. Nothing was considered too weird or bizarre; everything was given serious thought and, if at all possible, tried.

This probing, which involved extensive research, analysis, and experimentation, in most cases resulted in my coming right back full circle to the old tried-and-true ways. Nevertheless, now and then I come across some worthwhile variations, and slowly over the years my gardening approach did undergo certain changes.

The thought processes that reshaped my perception of gardening, along with their results, are presented here.

A bit of gardening philosophy

Generally, when something is very complicated, the tendency is to analyze then simplify: Most of the time this is a good idea. But, with the growing of plants simpler is not always better. In nature complexity is essential to maintain stability. Simple systems are very erratic. In regions where there are few species of insects and plants there will be severe changeability.

If, for instance, insect A has only a single predator, if that one stops reproducing, there will not be anything to keep insect A in check. It will soon multiply out of control.

In a complex ecosystem there are many predators for any one insect. If one predator is eliminated, nothing drastic changes because the others are still there to maintain the balance.

Just as a diversity of insects ensures stability so does a complex plant population. A bug that eats one plant may not eat any other. A diversified planting in itself acts as a natural check.

What's more, the plants that bug does not eat may be the place where his predators go to breed, as different plants appeal to different insects. Complexity is desirable; don't try to figure out all of the workings of nature, just accept it.

If one takes time to observe, one will notice many instances of why the complex ecosystem is best. I have found that gardening is less stressful and more successful if one makes the effort to learn from, and cooperate with, Mother Nature.

In nature there is always a variety of plants growing side by side. It is not natural for just one species to grow over a large area all by itself. If this begins to happen, a disease, a swarm of locusts, or something else will develop to devastate the plants and restore the balance.

This principle can and should be applied to the home garden. Monoculture should be avoided: as in nature, create diversity. There should always be a variety of vegetables growing in close proximity to each other. This will lessen the chances of disease or insect problems.

As for weeds in the garden, they are simply plants trying to reclaim their own territory. They have a right to be there and are helpful and beneficial up to a point. They are much stronger than the garden plants and will come up first, breaking the soil and helping to keep it from crusting. Don't be too quick to pull them, let them help you first!

Just as I understand the right of weeds to grow, I am also aware that insects have the right to exist. They are an important part of nature, each contributing something and each having a natural enemy. In other words, unless the balance of nature is upset, they usually are not a great problem. It is not possible or desirable to completely eliminate all bugs from a garden. The goal should not be eradication, it should be control.

The first control is to grow healthy plants. Vigorous plants will not be bothered much by bugs.

The second control is not to grow plants that seem to attract an unusual amount of insects. For some reason perhaps that plant is not suited to your area or to your soil.

The third control is garden hygiene. Bugs are attracted by rotting vegetation or dying plants. Keep the garden clean, pick up any fallen leaves, fruit, or other debris. Remove any diseased or dying plants promptly.

The fourth control is to avoid monoculture. It is nature's way and it does work. An inordinate amount of harmful insects are not attracted to mixed plantings.

As for soil, it has been my observation that nature does not tolerate bare earth. Something must either be growing on it or covering it at all times. If a patch of ground is suddenly exposed by an unusual occurrence, very quickly some type of plant life will start to grow there. Aside from any abnormal circumstance, in nature the soil remains intact from season to season; there is no disruption in its structure equivalent to the gardener turning the soil every year.

While digging up the ground is necessary in the establishment of a new garden, once the soil is in good tilth it does more harm than good. In the fall nature covers the ground with falling leaves and other decaying material. Following that lead, at the end of the growing season, in preparation for winter, I cover the bare ground with a mulch of leaves. Mother Nature does not dig up the earth every year, so now, neither do I. After all, Mother knows best!

Having said all that, it must always be kept in mind that a vegetable garden is an introduction of alien plants, an upsetting of the natural balance in that plot of ground. Nature will continually try to eradicate it.

Therefore, on some occasions, the gardener will be compelled to fight nature, while in other instances it is better to let her have her way. It is a delicate balancing act.

As for soil management, there is no question that Mother Nature's methods are best. Improve the soil using only organic methods: absolutely no pesticides, no artificial fertilizers or chemicals of any kind.

In the case of insect control one can go along to a certain extent. However, complete reliance on nature in this area is not practical as there will always be times when the natural enemies of a bug that is chewing on your crops are either out of town or otherwise occupied. On such occasions you are the only natural enemy of this bug available. At other times there may be an unusual influx of a particular type of insect. Again, you cannot sit idly by; you must act to bring the situation under control: the key word being "control," not necessarily total annihilation.

As for weeds, again, nature cannot be allowed to dominate completely, accept them as long as they are serving a beneficial purpose, beyond that point they have to be eliminated.

We must always be aware that we are presiding over an altered environment; nature's ways will have to be slightly modified to be compatible. In the real world we have to face realities, and the reality is that we cannot grow vegetables successfully simply by letting nature take its course. The time tested methods of conventional gardening cannot be dismissed lightly, they still have an important role in gardening.

All things considered, I have reached the conclusion that combining natural methods with conventional methods is the logical road to take. It is the road that I have chosen and have been rewarded with gratifying results.

Gardening economics

When we establish a home garden we are, basically, in the business of growing vegetables. Whether the produce is sold or not, is irrelevant, something of monetary worth is being produced. To be a feasible venture, the total value of vegetables produced must be more than total expenses. If a garden is viewed from that perspective, it is obvious that costs must be kept to an absolute minimum.

As in a new commercial enterprise a written "business plan" is a big help in creating a no-nonsense vegetable garden. The benefit of such a plan is that by putting it down on paper you can see the whole picture.

It also forces you to think things through, making it less likely to overlook something very important.

The "business plan" for establishing my garden was a clear specific listing of goals. Once those had been set then I could concentrate on the exact size, configuration, and method of working the garden. During that phase, there were many mistakes and detours. I constantly had to refer back to my recorded objectives to get back on track.

Many seasons went by before I was able to integrate organic growing methods and my modular system into an effective unit. This combination meets all of the economic requirements as it is efficient, productive, and cheap.

To establish a three-module home vegetable garden there are certain unavoidable start-up costs; basic tools, watering devices, and the materials for making all of the modular components must be bought. But, these are usually only one-time expenses; most of these items, if properly cared for, will last a lifetime.

Beyond those initial expenditures, with the use of organic growing methods, year to year expenses are very low. Compost is made at no cost, no outlay of cash is needed for leaf mulches, and earthworms work for nothing.

Practicing frugality in gardening simply makes good common sense. Unnecessary expenditures are never justified: the less your costs, the greater the value of the produce.

Starting my new garden: the trials, errors, and successes
My search for a better way of growing vegetables that, among other things, led to the development of my modular gardening system was a long but fulfilling journey.

The first step of this endeavor came about, when due to the requirements of a growing family, I bought a modest house that had a small backyard. Although just about everyone else on the block was concerned about having a perfect front lawn, it was the area in the back of the house that aroused my interest. I hadn't done any gardening since my teens. But looking back there my mind visualized row after row of vegetables.

I began to take note of the patterns of sunshine and shade to determine the best place to start a garden. It wasn't long before that became apparent. A spot a few feet from the garage wall received sun most of the day and the sun's rays bouncing off the concrete block wall warmed up that area earlier in the spring.

Size was a key factor. Enough room had to be left for other activities and, being employed in a full time job, ongoing upkeep was a big consideration. It had to be fairly small. But still, it was unthinkable to have a make-believe garden, just something as a part-time hobby to putter around in. If I was going to have a garden, it was going to be a serious garden, one with purpose, one from which a family could harvest a meaningful amount of produce.

Along that same vein of thought, it had to be cost effective. If it would cost more to raise vegetables than to buy them at the supermarket, that wouldn't be acceptable. The garden had to offset its costs and in effect make a "profit."

All of this brainstorming gradually clarified the objectives to the point where it was time to stop dreaming and start doing. I bought a notebook to use as a garden diary and entered the goals. The garden had to be:

    1) Fairly small.
    2) Manageable by one person.
    3) Productive.
    4) Cost effective.

The standards were set, this was the criterion. The next step was to attempt to translate the concept into reality—the actual establishment of the garden.

Evolution of the modular garden

I now knew where the garden was going to be located; the sunny spot by the garage wall was perfect. But I didn't want to just indiscriminately start digging.

Certain aspects had to be considered. It shouldn't dominate the yard and it shouldn't look like an open sore in the grass. Further, my children played back there, and kids being kids, thought had to be given to lessening the probability of them running all over it.

I had just read a book on French intensive gardening, a system that uses raised beds. The raised beds have the advantage of prolonging the season and promoting soil warmth and drainage. They also allow for close spacing of plants, a very important issue where gardening area is limited.

The merits of raised beds seemed to be unquestionable. Without a second thought I decided to create my garden in that form. As for the possibility of my children running into the beds, I reasoned that if framed with lumber they would be identified as gardens and not be disturbed. Looking back, I cannot recollect seeing any footprints in the beds, so it would seem that my logic was correct (although I can't really be certain).

Since more that one bed would be needed, it seemed logical to make them in a modular form, all the exact same size. As a graphic designer I had used the principles of modular design many times in my work.

Modular design involves the use of modules to accomplish an objective. Modules are exact identical units, each interchangeable with any another. For example, a brick is a module, each is exactly the same, and if used together in different combinations, a wide variety of structures can be built.

Determining the size of the modules was easy. Since standard-size lumber comes in 8-foot lengths, 4 feet by 8 feet was the answer. This size requires only three 8-foot 2x4s for each module (one being cut in half). This size is also a convenient size to work. The bed can be easily reached into from all sides.

Note: Standard-sized 8-foot-length lumber is sometimes slightly longer than 8 feet. If excessive, trim as necessary.

The area that had been selected would accommodate three 4- by 8-foot plots with enough room for 2-foot pathways between. Pathways are necessary because the beds should never be stepped into. They also act as barriers against soilborne diseases, preventing their spread from one module to another.

Early one morning the area was measured and, using a long-handled shovel, the 4- by 8-foot raised beds were double dug. They were then framed with 2x4 lumber. The sod was retained in the 2-foot pathways. By the end of the day the three-module vegetable garden was established and it looked good. With grass all around and in between on the pathways it blended in well with its surroundings. I was pleased with the results.

As per my criterion, I started out small, but as my enthusiasm grew, so did the size of my garden. It wasn't long before I began adding modules. I became obsessed with attempting to grow every type of vegetable that existed. I read gardening book after gardening book, trying all of their "tips," as well as all of their conventional, unconventional, and some just plain crazy gardening techniques.

About five years later, the garden had become much too big for me to keep up with. It had grown to double the size and took up more than half of the yard. Clearly I had strayed too far from my original criterion.

It was time to rethink and get back to the basic concept of a small garden manageable by one person.

To start, half modules were eliminated; then full modules. As modules were done away with, by necessity, the number of crops grown had to be reduced. A reevaluation was in order.

Obviously, in a smaller garden, priority had to be given to crops that gave the greatest yield for space and effort. These were: lettuce, bush beans, beets, carrots, and tomatoes. All were vegetables much used by my family. They definitely had to stay.

Those being set, then came the painful process of culling. To avoid eliminating any more than was absolutely necessary, succession plantings were increased. This had the added benefit of prolonging the harvest season.

But, even with this, hard decisions still remained. Each new season I would reevaluate. One of the first to go was celery, with no regrets. Then corn, with many regrets. Celery had always been a difficult crop, causing much frustration and little yield. Corn was another matter. Store-bought corn can never match the sweetness of the freshly picked homegrown. I still miss it, but it simply required too much room.

As season followed season, more difficult choices. Spinach, like corn, is another crop that has a tremendous difference in taste between homegrown and commercially grown. But facts had to be faced. It was always a problem crop, requiring precise timing, a lot of nourishment, and a quick bolting to seed the minute that the days began to lengthen. A lot of work for little in return: To drop or not to drop? My taste buds said no, but my brain said yes. Logic had to prevail. Spinach was dropped.

Now real progress was being made. The next year, zucchini with its sprawling growth was out, this was followed by the dropping of potatoes. The elimination of these two space hogs allowed for the introduction of broccoli into the garden, an easy to grow crop harvestable up into late fall.

As the garden was beginning to get down to a manageable size, one thing that became apparent was that much too much lettuce was being planted. About half of it was bolting to seed unharvested. By cutting back on it, I was able to add Swiss chard and parsley: Two excellent additions. Both are long season crops. Both are very productive, and Swiss chard holds up in hot weather, furnishing salad bowl material when lettuce has just about run its course.

At this point, finally, the selection of what crops to grow was just about settled and my garden had shrunk back to my original three modules.

The smaller garden enabled me to notice details that had previously been overlooked. In a large garden there is room for error, if for any reason a few plants are lost, it is of no great concern. In a small garden efficiency is of paramount importance, every plant counts.

I began to experiment with different spacing between rows to see if more plants could be grown in a given area. Distances were varied between lettuce plants, some being spaced 6 inches apart, others 8 or 10 inches, trying to determine the optimum spacing. Other crops were handled in the same way.

Crop rotation also had to be reconsidered. With all of the changes, the old rotation was no longer applicable. Plus, two plantings a season were now being made in every bed: an initial planting in the spring followed by a succession planting later.

Not only did rotation from year to year have to be taken into consideration but also from initial plantings to succession plantings. A valid sequence had to be maintained throughout, within the season as well as from season to season. Not an easy thing to do—in fact it presented a real challenge.

The problem was addressed by spending many hours planning on paper what crops would be planted in what module. I just continued to move crops around until I arrived at what seemed to be the right mix.

At the same time my attention again returned to row spacing, trying to find a standard. Was it possible to find a "one-size-fits-all" solution? Over the years, measurements that are based on

2-inch increments were gradually arrived at. Spacing of rows is measured using multiplies of that increment.

After much trial and error, an area measuring 16 inches down the side of the module by the module width was found to be about the average space needed for any one planting. A module is 8 feet long (96 inches). When it is divided by 16 inches, it results in six 16- by 48-inch units (16- by 45-inch soil area). Since these "modules within a module" are the areas to be planted, logically enough, I call them "planting units." A shallow saw mark was made at these points on both sides of the frame to identify them. Then between these marks, as a guide to row spacing, at 4-inch intervals 1¼-inch galvanized nails were driven.

The minimum space devoted to a crop is one half of a planting unit. The maximum space available in a module is, of course, the full module, six planting units.

These planting units helped greatly in planning sowings and crop rotation. In the winter months this became my favorite pastime, drawing up different possibilities of plantings and rotations; then evaluating the merits of each.

When all the planning and evaluating was completed, I felt that, finally, I had achieved the criterion that was initially set.

The garden was:

1) Fairly small. The garden consisted of three 4- by 8-foot modules. Lined up side by side with 2-foot pathways between, this occupied a space of 8 feet by 16 feet.

2) Manageable by one person. I was able to maintain it without difficulty. Depending on what had to be done, about a half hour or so after work on weekdays and a hour or two, or three, or four, or more, on weekends took care of all that had to be done.

3) Productive. The selection of vegetables was such that a long harvest was obtained, starting with cool weather crops in the spring, continuing with warm weather crops through the summer, and then finishing up with cool weather crops again into the late fall.

4) Cost effective. After the initial cost for lumber and tools, the only recurring cost was for seed and water. (Seed and water costs can be reduced by saving some of your own seed and using barrels to collect rainwater.)

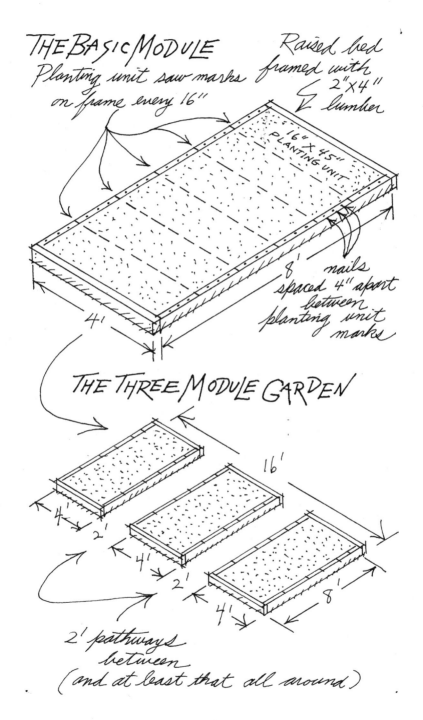

THE BASIC MODULE
Planting unit saw marks
on frame every 16"

Raised bed
framed with
2"x4"
lumber

16" X 45"
PLANTING UNIT

8'   nails
spaced 4" apart
between
planting unit
marks

4'

THE THREE MODULE GARDEN

16'

4'
2'

4'
2'

4'

8'

2' pathways
between
(and at least that all around)

2

The three-module garden

Three 4- by 8-foot modules lined up side by side, leaving 2-foot pathways between, measures 8 feet by 16 feet, plus 2 feet of space all around, equals 12 feet by 20 feet, the area needed to accommodate a side by side three-module garden

Locating the three module garden

The choice of a location will require some thought. Take the time to carefully analyze the site.

The first three most important things are *Sunshine, Sunshine, Sunshine.* This cannot be stressed enough. Sunshine is of primary importance, the garden must be located where it will get a minimum of 6 to 8 hours of sunlight a day.

Soil condition is of secondary significance as it can always be improved. Anyway, generally, in a backyard there is not much difference in this respect from one spot to another. But be sure that the area is free of roots from trees or large bushes.

Good air circulation helps plants breathe, grow better, and helps prevent diseases. Avoid any sites too closed in.

Drainage is another aspect to consider. When it rains, check to see if there are any areas where the water puddles up. Stay away from those places if you can.

Lastly, *it should not be too far away from the house or a water supply.* Otherwise it probably will be neglected.

But you shouldn't worry too much about finding the perfect spot for the garden, it may not exist. Most of us, not having a lot of land, have very little choice about where the garden is to go.

Some people like to do the location planning on paper before doing any digging, but if making sketches is not your cup of tea just make the three frames and procedure as follows:

First: Go to pages 24 and 25 and follow the instructions of how to make the frames. Then, once the frames have been completed, place them on the ground in the area (or areas) that you have chosen. Keep in mind that the garden will be easier to care for if they are close to each other. When placed side by side all maintenance will be simpler. But if for some reason that is not possible, position them wherever they need to be to fit the limitations of your lot.

Then for the next few days walk around them and generally observe them. Do they get enough sun? Are they far enough away from trees or fences? Is there at least 2 feet of room all around?

When you are completely satisfied, drive a small stake into the ground at each inside corner to mark their position. Then set them aside so that they will not interfere with the digging.

Making the raised beds

Once the locations of the modules have been determined, the making of the raised beds can be started.

The best time of year to do this is in the fall. This allows the digging, aerating, and adding of organic material to the soil far enough in advance of planting to, through weathering, improve the soil structure. In the spring the soil will be ready for planting after a few rakings. If it is not possible to do this in the fall, then the next best time is in the spring, as early as possible.

Whenever, fall or spring, avoid working the soil when it is wet and sticks together excessively. If dug at these times the soil will tend to form clods. Before you dig, test it. Pick up a handful of the soil and squeeze it into a ball. Press this ball with a forefinger, it should crumble. If it does, it is ready for digging. If it doesn't, the soil is still too wet.

Before you start, gather as much organic material as you can: leaves, crop residues, dried weeds, hedge trimmings, and similar materials. The more that you can incorporate into the soil at this time the better. This is an opportunity to improve the tilth of the soil.

If you are starting the garden in a grassy area, establishing it will be easier if the sod is smothered out. Mow the grass very close, then cover with a thick layer of newspapers, cardboard, large brown grocery bags, or anything else that will block out the sun. It will take several months to smother out the grass.

Double digging

The raised bed is basically made by loosening up the soil to create air pockets. The adding of organic material further helps to fluff it up. The spade work is done by the time-honored practice of double digging. It is a bit of work, but in establishing the modular garden it usually needs to be done only once.

When digging, try not to invert the soil, the top soil should remain on top. Throw each shovelful forward so that the natural layering of the soil remains. (If digging in sod, it has to be turned over, there is no choice.)

1) To begin, using a long-handled pointed shovel, start at one end of a measured 4- by 8-foot plot. Dig a trench a shovel blade deep by about a foot wide across the four foot width. Deposit the removed soil beyond the other end. You will need this soil to fill the last trench.

2) Then standing on the untouched part of the bed, dig the shovel down another blade depth (or as far as you can go). Leave it there and lever the handle down, then return it to the vertical position. Repeat this levering back and forth several times to loosen the subsoil. Remove the shovel, move a blade width over, and repeat this procedure all the way across the trench.

3) When this has been completed, place organic material in the far side of the trench as vertically as possible.

4) Then dig a second trench behind the first one throwing the soil forward to mix with the organic material. (If digging in sod, turn the spade-full over and give it a whack to crumble it.) Repeat the loosening of the subsoil with the shovel as was done in the first trench, then add the organic material.

5) Dig a third trench and so on, repeating the procedure until the whole bed is dug. Shovel the soil that was moved to the back into the last trench. That will complete the bed.

Once the bed has been prepared, do not step on it. This would compact the soil and adversely affect plant growth. The beds won't have too much height the first year. But you can slowly

MAKING A RAISED BED

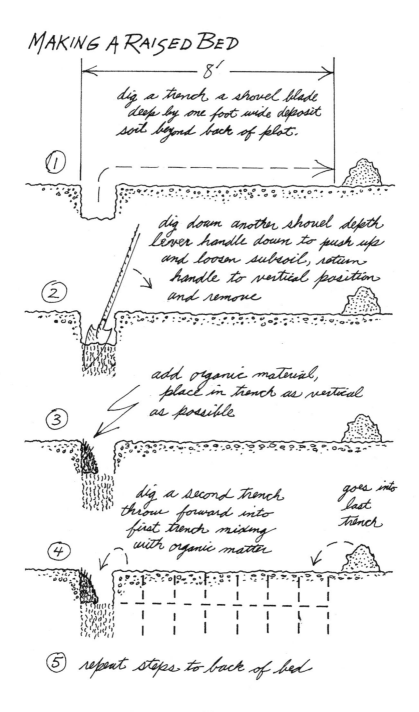

8'

① dig a trench a shovel blade deep by one foot wide deposit soil beyond back of plot.

② dig down another shovel depth lever handle down to push up and loosen subsoil, return handle to vertical position and remove

③ add organic material, place in trench as vertical as possible

④ dig a second trench throw forward into first trench mixing with organic matter

goes into last trench

⑤ repeat steps to back of bed

23

build them up a little at a time. This double digging and the adding of organic material may have to be repeated the first few years of a new garden until the beds are in good tilth.

When the double digging of all three beds has been completed, they can then be framed.

Making the frames

Standard-size lumber is used, three 8-foot 2x4s for each frame. Two 8-foot 2x4s remain intact to form the sides. Cut the third one in half to make the ends. Nail the 4-foot ends onto the 8-foot sides to form a rectangle. Use two 20D 4-inch galvanized nails at each corner. Next; measure off 16-inch increments on the tops of both sides to indicate the planting units. Make a shallow saw cut across these points so that they will be permanent. Then, as row spacing guides, in-between those marks, just drive a 3D 1¼-inch galvanized nail at 4-inch intervals.

The frame is then complete. To place them down to encase the raised beds, you probably will have to remove a little soil from all sides with a garden trowel. Remove as needed so that the frame goes down easily without disturbing the bed too much. Once all three are in place, check again to make sure that the pathways between them are at least 2 feet wide. If you are completely satisfied and feel comfortable walking around them, drive a stake at the center of the sides and ends to keep them from moving. Put back any soil that was removed earlier.

When the 4-foot ends of the frame are nailed to the 8-foot sides their thickness increases that dimension by 3 inches. This makes the actual overall outside dimensions of the frame 4 feet by 8 feet, 3 inches, but in the interest of simplicity I have been calling them 4- by 8-foot modules and will continue to do so.

After the raised beds have been made and framed, the three-module garden is complete and ready for use. But, before getting into gardening procedures, a few words about the items needed to carry out these procedures.

Gardening tools and equipment

In this section the items needed are described and illustrated. If the listing seems exceptionally "bare bones," that is because it is. Don't waste money on things that you don't need.

FRAME FOR RAISED BED

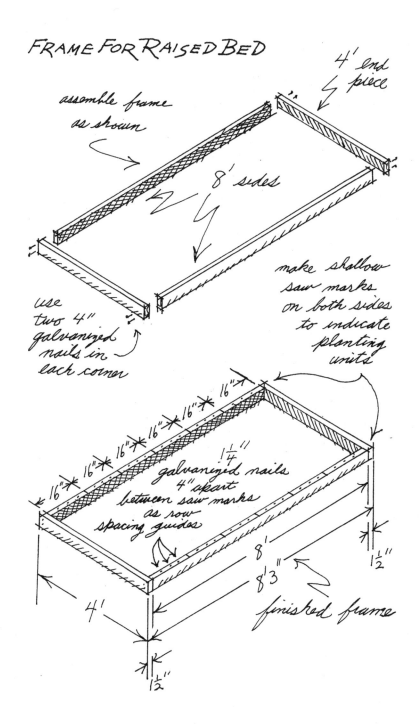

4' end piece

assemble frame as shown

8' sides

use two 4" galvanized nails in each corner

make shallow saw marks on both sides to indicate planting units

16" 16" 16" 16" 16" 16" 16" 16"

$1\frac{1}{4}$" galvanized nails 4" apart between saw marks as row spacing guides

8'

8' 3"

$1\frac{1}{2}$"

4'

$1\frac{1}{2}$"

finished frame

25

The modular planting stick
I have designed a planting stick specifically to be used with the modular gardening system. It is made using a 4-foot length of 1x2 lumber: First, it is painted white; then small pencil marks are made in 1-inch increments along both edges. Starting from one end, using a ballpoint pen and a straight edge, at every fourth mark a line is drawn all the way across the stick. Next, at the marks in-between those, draw a ³⁄₈-inch-long line on both edges. Then in-between those, a ¹⁄₈-inch-long line is drawn. To indicate the center point a 1-inch-long line is drawn perpendicular to and crossing the line in the center of the stick.

At planting time this is the only measuring device needed, no strings, stakes, or tape measures to complicate matters.

Gardening tools and watering devices
To work the garden you will need only the basics. They are readily available anywhere gardening supplies are sold.

Long-handled pointed shovel: The point is important as it makes it easy to penetrate the soil. The long handle gives leverage, requiring less effort. It is essential in establishing a new garden, but once the garden is established it is seldom used.

Rake: The rake is indispensable for leveling off and preparing a seedbed. Also used for taking up the mulch in early spring and tamping down after sowing peas. In addition it performs a variety of tasks—the workhorse of my garden.

Hand trowel: The hand trowel is used for transplanting and for a wide variety of other small digging tasks.

Hand cultivator: The hand cultivator is used to break up any crusting of the soil and to keep it loose.

Hose, impulse sprinkler, watering wand: The impulse sprinkler puts out a fine mist and is used for freshly seeded plots. The watering wand can be adjusted from a spray to a stream and is used mostly for established plants.

Watering can: If one does not have the facilities for the use of a hose then a watering can will be required.

Even if you have a hose many times a watering can is quicker and easier to use. Every gardener should have one. The old standby is the classic galvanized model, but the plastic ones are a lot cheaper and will do the job just as well.

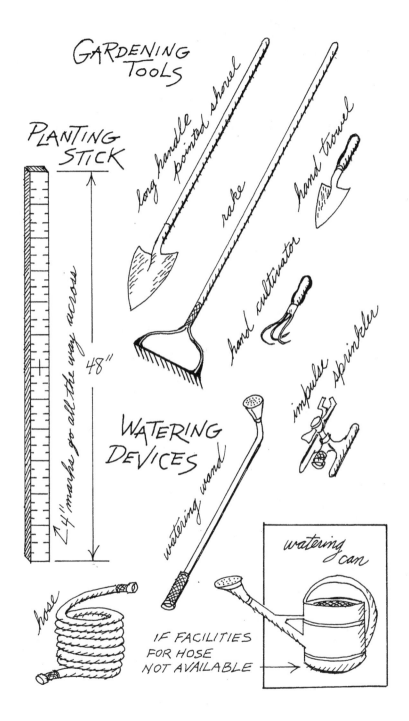

GARDENING TOOLS

PLANTING STICK

long handle pointed shovel

rake

hand trowel

hand cultivator

impulse sprinkler

2 4" marks go all the way across

48"

WATERING DEVICES

watering wand

hose

watering can

IF FACILITIES FOR HOSE NOT AVAILABLE →

3

Gardening procedures

Since the modular garden is a little different, so are some of its procedures. All rows are 4 feet long, parallel with the module width, and are measured out utilizing the indicators on the frames. All furrows are made using the planting stick.

The procedures described here generally apply in most situations. Any deviations will be given in the individual vegetable planting instructions later in the book.

Soil structure
In order to properly work and water the soil one should have a basic knowledge of its structure.

Healthy soil is a living substance; it is filled with bacteria and microorganisms that break down organic matter and make their nutrients available to plants.

The size of soil particles determines its classification. Most garden soils are classified as sandy, clayey, or loamy. There are also soils that are comprised of silt, but these are very rare. Silt is usually a minor ingredient in other soils.

Sand particles are large and feel rough and gritty. Their large size keeps them from packing together tightly, which results in a lot of open spaces between particles. This means that there is a lot of air in the soil and much room for roots to expand. On the other hand, this also means that water goes through these spaces very quickly. It doesn't hold moisture very long. Sand warms up quickly and does not compact to mud in wet weather. It is easily worked but provides poor anchorage for plant roots: excellent for root crops, especially carrots.

Clay particles are very fine, so small that they cannot be seen by the naked eye. Yellow in color, clay is a common ingredient in many soils. It is the opposite of sandy soil. The particles are tightly packed; there is very little air space between them. Air, water, and roots have a hard time penetrating. Clayey soils drain poorly, are slow to dry out, and when completely dry will be as hard as a brick. When wet, they are sticky and difficult to work. They are very prone to compaction.

Loam is a composition of sand, clay, and silt. (Silt is akin to clay, but particles are a little larger.) Usually, loam also contains some organic matter. The soil particles of loam are large enough to allow adequate air spaces. Water and plant roots penetrate readily. It drains well, but at the same time holds moisture. It works fairly easily and is pretty much the ideal garden soil.

Many soils are mixtures, some perhaps even defying an exact classification. Whatever your soil type, it is what you are stuck with. Fortunately any soil can be considerable improved by the addition of organic matter.

Soil preparation
Soil preparation is one of the most important steps in gardening. If one is to have the loose friable soil necessary to make a fine seedbed, the work must be started in the fall.

If starting a new garden, this means that the earth must be double dug, incorporating as much organic material as possible. A lot of work, but necessary: Furthermore, you may have to repeat this for the next several years before the soil is in an acceptable condition. It all depends on a lot of different factors.

In an established garden, the procedure in the fall is very different. The earth is no longer dug up. Instead, after all crops, weeds, and other residues have been cleared, the soil is given a shallow cultivation with a rake.

Let it lie bare for the next several weeks. Then put down a 3- to 4-inch mulch of shredded leaves. This mulch will protect the earth, keep the moisture in, and allow the soil life to continue uninterrupted through the winter, giving the earthworms the bottom decomposing leaves to feast on, which adds humus to the soil.

SOIL STRUCTURE

GET TO KNOW YOUR SOIL

plant roots grow in the *air* spaces between soil particles

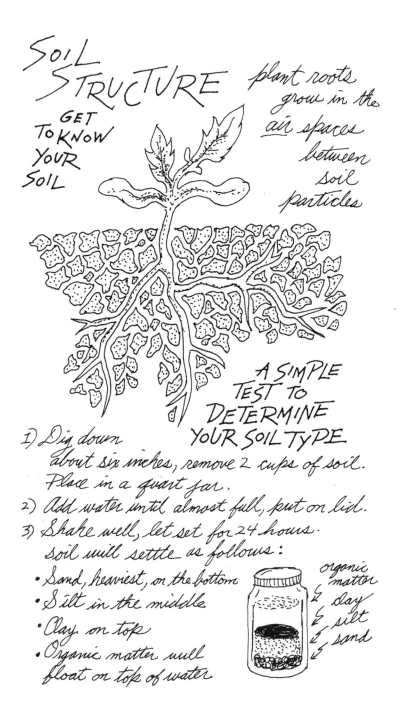

A SIMPLE TEST TO DETERMINE YOUR SOIL TYPE

1) Dig down about six inches, remove 2 cups of soil. Place in a quart jar.
2) Add water until almost full, put on lid.
3) Shake well, let set for 24 hours. soil will settle as follows:
   - Sand, heaviest, on the bottom
   - Silt in the middle
   - Clay on top
   - Organic matter will float on top of water

organic matter
clay
silt
sand

30

Depending on the weather, about two or three weeks before the earliest spring planting date, remove the mulch. Make a preliminary shallow cultivation with a rake to kill any larvae that may have overwintered. Level off the soil, then leave bare. Do not work the soil any further at this point; it should not be worked any more than necessary too far in advance of the time of the actual planting.

Preparing the seedbed

The preparation of the seedbed should be done right before the actual planting. Give another raking to uproot any weeds that may have sprouted, to smooth out any lumps, and to mix the drier surface soil with the moist soil underneath.

For the large seed vegetables that is all that has to be done. Sow the seed before the soil starts to dry out.

For small seed vegetables the soil needs to be a bit finer. The density has to be such that the soil will make close contact with the seeds after firming down to ensure rapid germination.

Therefore for small seed plantings, immediately after the raking described above, go over the area again with the rake, smoothing and fining. It may be necessary to rake in several different directions, more than once, to achieve this fine seedbed. At this point, if available, spread a thin layer of fine compost over the entire area. Do not delay, sow the seed.

There are two plantings per season in the modular garden. The foregoing describes the procedure for the initial planting.

The succession planting procedure is very much the same. The main difference is that in each planting unit, or units, where there has been an initial planting, that crop has to be fully harvested before you can proceed. Then, all remnants of the initial planting must be removed, the soil cleared, raked, and left bare until time for the succession planting. This in-between phase is usually a very short period.

As in the initial planting, for large seed vegetables and transplants just give a second light raking right before planting.

For small seed vegetables, also give a second light raking, but the soil needs to be broken down a bit more. Spend some extra time to make a fine seedbed. Again, for small seed, it is best to spread a thin layer of fine compost over the area.

Laying out the rows
The nail heads and saw marks on the frame are the row spacing guides. You can mark where the rows are to go by just poking a forefinger in the ground at the proper points.

Making the furrows
When the spacing of the rows have been determined, lay the planting stick across the module so that each end is touching the correct nail head, or saw mark. Then turn the stick to a 45-degree angle so that the edge facing the soil points straight down. When pressed into the soil at this angle the stick will make a "V"-shape furrow. Work the stick back and forth across the module until a furrow is made to the proper depth.

If the soil is below the top edge of the frame, the stick will not make contact with the ground. In that case an "auxiliary planting stick" will have to be made. This is simply a 36-inch length of 1x2 lumber. This length will fit within the sides of the frame. Holding the planting stick flat in position with one hand, with the other, place the auxiliary stick against it and tilt to a 45-degree angle, then work back and forth to make the furrow.

For small seeds make a shallow furrow, usually about ¼ inch deep. For large seeds the furrows need to be a little deeper, about 1 inch to 1½ inch deep. Plus, in some cases the large seeds may have to be pushed further into the soil with a forefinger to get the right depth. But do not plant too deep.

As a general rule of thumb, the deeper you plant them, the longer it will take them to germinate and come up.

Plant spacing
Plants are spaced relative to each other in different ways, which can determine to a large extent how they will develop. In a vegetable garden the object is to grow plants of high quality, getting maximum yield from the area used.

Each plant has an optimum spacing. They need good air movement around them, but not to an extreme. Plants also seem to need the close, but not too close, companionship of their own species. If too far apart they will suffer extra exposure to harsh weather and more earth will be bare causing loss of soil moisture. Development will be uneven, weed growth will be greater, and

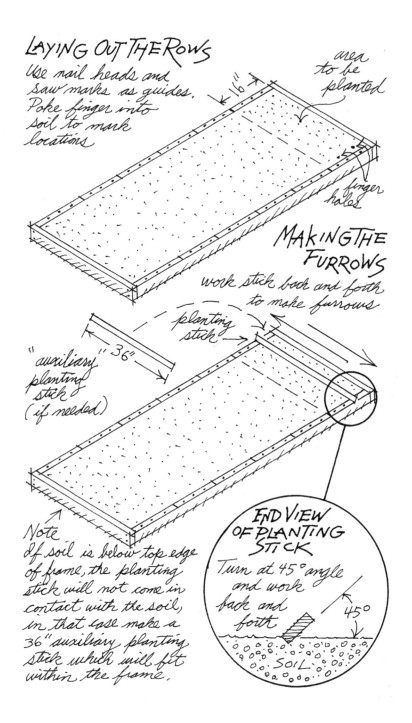

LAYING OUT THE ROWS

Use nail heads and saw marks as guides. Poke finger into soil to mark locations

16"

area to be planted

finger holes

MAKING THE FURROWS

work stick back and forth to make furrows

"auxiliary" planting stick (if needed)

36"

planting stick

Note

If soil is below top edge of frame, the planting stick will not come in contact with the soil, in that case make a 36" auxiliary planting stick which will fit within the frame.

END VIEW OF PLANTING STICK

Turn at 45° angle and work back and forth

45°

SOIL

production will be less. Too close will also reduce yield. The intense increased competition and restricted air flow will cause stress and unhealthy conditions conducive to pests and diseases.

That being said, a middle ground of reasonably close planting provides a mini-climate and a living mulch. It reduces weed growth and helps hold moisture in the soil. This will usually mean smaller plants.

But this does not necessarily mean lower yield; because there are more plants the overall yield can be greater. For that reason, each vegetable has to be analyzed as to its individual characteristics, the space available, and any practicalities before determining its spacing.

Conventional rows
Traditionally, plants are spaced a set distance within rows and rows are spaced a set greater distance apart. This means that they will line up not only within the rows but also with the plants in parallel rows: more or less like soldiers in their ranks.

In the conventional garden, due to the need of walking room, rows are very far apart. This is not a factor with the raised beds since they are never stepped into. Therefore other considerations are used to determine planting distances. There is no reason for huge spaces between rows.

Staggered rows
This scheme is similar to sowing in conventional rows. The difference is that, although plants line up within the rows, they do not line up with the plants in adjacent rows. All seeds are spaced the same distance within each row, but the starting point is shifted in alternating rows so that they do not line up across. Instead they are placed at a midpoint.

This staggering allows the rows to be much closer to each other. Distances can be greater, the same, or even less than within row spacing.

Rows can be as little as one fourth the distances between the plants in the rows. Diagonally they will be equidistant; each will have exactly the same space around it. Theoretically this ensures equal benefits to all plants, as every one should get about the same amount of moisture, light, and nutrients that are available.

PLANT SPACING

The spacing relationship of plants to each other will determine to a large extent how they will develop

CONVENTIONAL ROWS
TYPICAL SEEDING PATTERN BELOW:

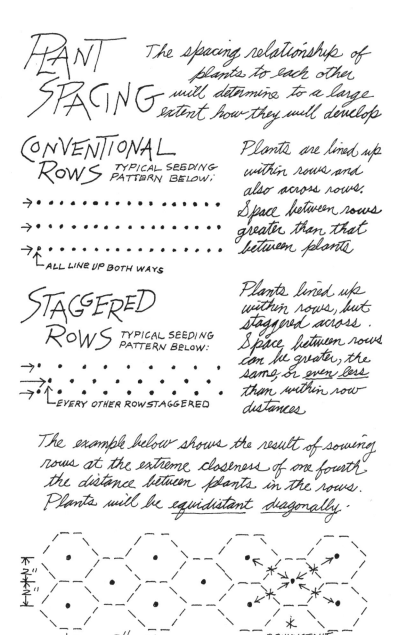

→ • • • • • • • • • • • • • • • •
→ • • • • • • • • • • • • • • • •
→ • • • • • • • • • • • • • • • •

└─ ALL LINE UP BOTH WAYS

Plants are lined up within rows and also across rows. Space between rows greater than that between plants

STAGGERED ROWS
TYPICAL SEEDING PATTERN BELOW:

→ • • • • • • • • •
→ • • • • • • • • •
→ • • • • • • • • •

└─ EVERY OTHER ROW STAGGERED

Plants lined up within rows, but staggered across. Space between rows can be greater, the same, or _even less_ than within row distances

The example below shows the result of sowing rows at the extreme closeness of one fourth the distance between plants in the rows. Plants will be _equidistant_ _diagonally_.

2"
2"

├─ 8" ─┤   EQUIDISTANT

Each plant, in theory, will have the same amount of space around it to draw nutrients.

35

CLUSTER PLANTING

Used mostly for large plants. Best, set in as transplants, rather than direct seeding.

"ON THE SQUARE"

SINGLE UNIT

COMBINED UNITS

Plants are in blocks. Each equidistant from each other, _horizontally_ and _vertically_

"ON THE DIAGONAL"

SINGLE UNIT

COMBINED UNITS

Plants are equidistant _diagonally_.

UNSTRUCTURED PLANTING — NO SET CRITERION

Plants are spaced using personal judgement

BROADCASTING — RANDOM SPACES

Broadcasting seed is unstructured. Results are a wide variety of distances

Further, as the plants grow, foliage should just touch or overlap. This will, in effect, create an air mulch, shading the soil and keeping down the weeds.

Cluster planting

Used for very large plants: For this system use transplants. Direct seeding is neither practical nor reliable. Clusters are really segments of widely spaced rows. They are formed in two ways:

1) "On the square." Transplants are set in at the corners of a square, spaced the same both vertically and horizontally.

2) "On the diagonal." One transplant is set in at each corner of a square or rectangle and one more in the exact center. This will space all of them equidistant diagonally.

In both cases additional seedlings can be added on at the same spacing, extending the plantings. See diagrams on the facing page.

Unstructured spacing

No prescribed rules are followed; spacing is in an arbitrary manner depending on one's judgment. There are often situations where plants need to be fit into an area and there is no need for rows or other formal arrangements. Still, in these cases, the basic requirements for healthy growth must not be forgotten. Adequate ground and air space must be considered.

Broadcasting results in unstructured spacing. The results are unpredictable and upon germination distances between seedlings will vary greatly. It is sometimes used for a number of leaf crops such as lettuce and other greens when harvesting is done by cutting or pulling all plants at a young stage. Since none are allowed to grow to maturity, spacing is not that important. Peas are also often broadcast, as a dense stand is needed.

Other

Hill planting is the sowing of small groups of seeds with wide spaces between groups. Used mostly for vine crops.

Triplex rows

A triplex row is an innovation that I have developed, born out of the frustration of trying to figure out the best way to sow certain small-seed leaf vegetables, such as lettuce, endive, and arugula. I had gone back and forth from broadcasting to rows and vice versa. I was always torn between the two methods. Which was better? I agonized over this for many years; I could not make a definite decision.

Rows are more orderly, easier to weed, thin, and cultivate. But when lettuce seed was broadcast it seemed to germinate and grow faster. The closeness of the seedlings shaded the soil, keeping the moisture in.

Up to a point this closeness was an advantage and they grew quickly. However, once they passed the seedling stage this became a disadvantage; overcrowding became a real problem.

Conversely, when lettuce was sown in single rows it did very poorly. Too much soil was left bare and the sun, along with the wind, quickly dried it out, stressing the plants.

Since I could not make up my mind as to what method was best, I reasoned that if a technique could be developed combining the advantages of broadcasting with the advantages of rows that would be the solution.

After much trial and error—success! I now sow most small seed leaf vegetables in what I call "triplex rows." This method retains the beneficial aspects of broadcasting while having the discipline and order of rows.

The basic triplex row method
A "triplex row" is simply three very closely spaced rows (about 2 inches apart). The center row, which I call the "main row," is the only row in which plants are allowed to grow to maturity.

The two flanking rows are "nurse rows." Plants in these rows will not stand to maturity. Their function is twofold:

First: To "nurse" the main row plants along by shading the soil, holding the moisture in, keeping weed seeds from sprouting, and to act as a buffer from drying winds.

Second: To provide an early harvest. As soon as the plants in the nurse rows are big enough to eat they are pulled, as needed, until all have been completely harvested.

The main row plants are thinned as seedlings, harvested at semi-maturity by plucking the outer leaves, and at maturity by pulling, or cutting, the entire plant. Nurse row plants are all pulled at a

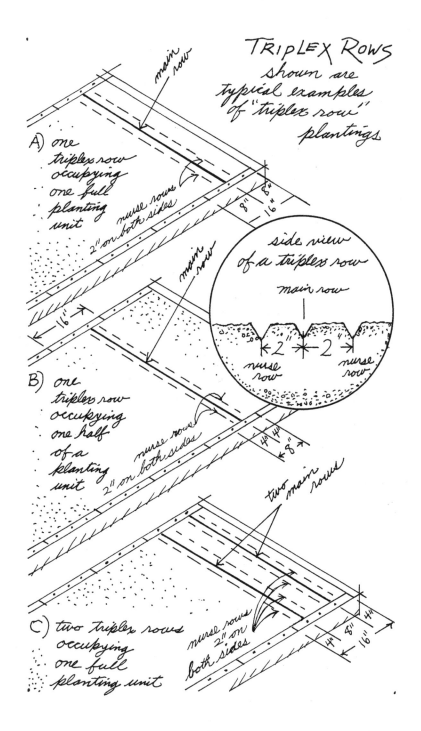

TRIPLEX ROWS
shown are typical examples of "triplex row" plantings

main row

A) one triplex row occupying one full planting unit

2" on both sides   nurse rows

8"
16"

16"

main row

side view of a triplex row

main row

2"   2"

nurse row   nurse row

B) one triplex row occupying one half of a planting unit

nurse rows   2" on both sides

4" 4"
8"

two main rows

C) two triplex rows occupying one full planting unit

nurse rows 2" on both sides

4" 8" 4"
16"

young stage giving early harvests. By the time both nurse rows have been fully harvested, the main row plants will be semi-mature and are harvested by plucking their outer leaves only. New leaves will grow back. Harvest main row plants when they elongate noticeably, a sign that they are ready to bolt to seed.

From the first thinnings to the final harvesting a steady supply of salad bowl material is always being produced.

The triplex row method is an important aspect of the modular garden. It provides optimum growing conditions for plants and is very productive as it makes a long harvest period possible from one sowing.

An additional benefit of this system is that the nurse row plants can be used to provide transplants to fill in any gaps that may have occurred in the main row.

The procedure for the making of a triplex row is as follows:

1) Determine the position of the main row. Then make that furrow first.

2) On both sides of this main row furrow, at a distance of about 2 inches (which is slightly more than the width of the planting stick), make two additional furrows. Lay the planting stick parallel to and next to one side of the main row furrow. Tilt the far edge to a 45-degree angle and make the nurse row furrow. Repeat on the other side.

3) If making two or more triplex rows, measure off the distances between main rows first. After making those main row furrows go back and make the nurse row furrows.

4) Sow the seed.

Cut-and-come-again triplex row method
This technique relies on the fact that many leafy crops will re-grow after being cut. Two, three, or more cuttings can be had from a single sowing. Harvesting is usually done at the large seedling or semi-mature stage. Used mostly for mesclun crops such as endive, arugula, lettuces, mustard, or similar. *(Mesclun is a French term for a mixture of young lettuces and greens.)*

Preparation and sowing is the same as in the basic triplex row method. Once germination takes place and seedlings have two or three true leaves, go over all rows and thin any clumps.

Usually, this is the only thinning necessary. There may be

situations later that develop when it will be obvious that some further thinning is needed.

Large seedling stage: Generally the first cut is made when the seedlings have developed six true leaves. Cut at least ½ inch above the base of the plant. New leaves usually will resprout from the stump within ten to fourteen days.

Semi-mature stage: Many plants such as endive can be cut when they are fairly large, but before they are mature. There is the option of cutting at the large seedling stage or waiting until later. The semi-mature cutting should be about 1 inch above the base. The bigger stump will make them put out a mass of fresh leaves, and even prevent them from bolting to seed prematurely.

Sowing the seed

As was discussed previously, seed can be sown in rows or by broadcasting. Each method has its pros and cons.

For small seed it is important to have a fine seedbed, to space properly, and to cover lightly. In fact some small seed need not be covered at all, just pressed into the soil.

For large seed the seedbed does not have to be as fine but it is important to space properly and not plant too deep: if properly spaced, it will require no thinning.

When covering both small and large seed, compost is recommended. You simply cannot overdo its use. Compost will help the soil maintain its moisture.

Large seed, sowing in single rows

For sowing large seed crops, there is no question, sowing in single rows is by far the best method. Peas are the only exception to this. Planting large seed crops in single rows facilitates cultivating, watering, and harvesting. The procedure is described starting below:

1) After the furrows have been made, take the planting stick and lay it alongside one of the furrows. Holding a small amount of seeds in one hand, pick them up with the other hand and, starting at the center mark, using the stick as a support, slide your hand toward you. Use the inch markings as a guide and drop a seed at the required distances.

2) When that furrow has been completed, move the stick

to the next furrow and sow as before. Continue until all of the furrows have been sown, then firm.

3) In some cases, it may be necessary to push the seed further into the soil with a forefinger to obtain the proper planting depth.

4) When all seed has been firmed, cover the furrows with the compost and water with a spray.

Small seed, sowing in single rows
While I sow all of my small-seed leaf vegetables in triplex rows, there are other small-seed crops that are sown in single rows. The techniques given apply in either case. With small seed, extra care must be taken to get an even spacing. Do not rush! The procedure is as follows:

1) After all furrows have been made, take the planting stick and lay it alongside one of the furrows.

2) The larger small seeds such as beets, Swiss chard, and radish are big enough so that the individual seeds can be picked up with the thumb and forefinger, then sown fairly accurately, using the planting stick markings as a guide.

3) Seeds smaller than those are a problem. They're too small to pick up individually with your fingers, and the best way to sow them eluded me season after season. It took a while, but eventually I did figure out a solution. All that is needed is a mailing envelope of any size and a ballpoint pen.

Take an envelope (one that you receive in the mail will do, no need to buy one). With a scissors, at a point of about 6 inches over from a bottom corner cut on an angle to a point about 3 inches up from that corner. The result will be a triangular shape that is open where cut and closed on the bottom and side. This is now your seed dispenser.

Take some small seed and pour it into the closed end of this dispenser. Place the bottom of the dispenser to rest in the very bottom of the "V" shaped furrow. Start with the pointed end at the center of the furrow. Hold the opposite closed end with one hand, your forefinger inside, thumb and middle finger outside. With the other hand use a ballpoint pen to push out a single seed. (A sharpened pencil or a small pointed stick can also be used.) Pulling the dispenser toward you, stop the

SOWING LARGE SEED

lay planting stick alongside of furrow, rest your hand on the stick for support using the markings as a guide, sow seed at the proper spacing

furrow

1) pick up the seed with thumb and forefinger
2) support your hand on the planting stick and drop seeds into furrow at correct distances

SOWING SMALL SEED

1) take any size envelope cut off a lower corner

2) put seed in back of this "dispenser"

APPROX 3"

APPROX 6"

3) pull towards you, push out one seed at a time with a ball point pen

4) curl forefinger push down firming the seed

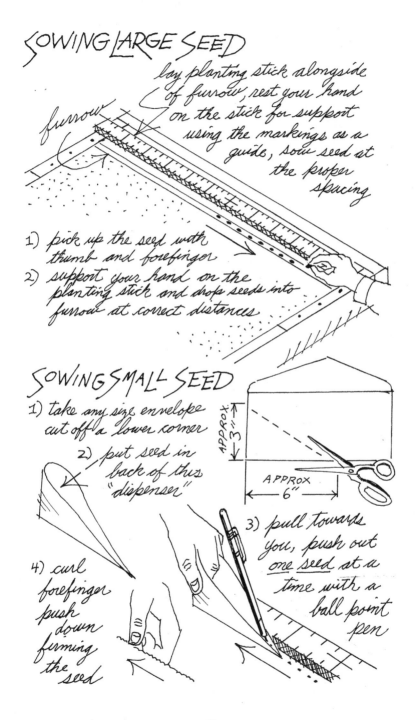

point at every inch mark on the planting stick and push out a seed. Finish sowing that half of the furrow, then repeat on the other half to complete the sowing.

4) Seed must be firmed, curl your forefinger and using the part between the first and second joints push down on the seed pressing it into the soil. The very small seed, usually, is best left uncovered. For the larger of the small seed, such as beet and radish, cover lightly with loose compost.

Sowing small seed is a bit tedious. The tendency is to get impatient and start to rush. But time spent now will pay off when the sprouts come up. Take a short break after doing each planting unit. Upon finishing all rows, water.

Small seed, sowing in triplex rows
Sowing seed for a triplex row is basically the same as sowing three single rows. The only difference being that the three furrows are very close together.

Begin by laying the planting stick alongside one of the nurse row furrows. Sow as described for single rows. Move the planting stick over to the main row furrow and sow it. Then, again moving the stick, sow the other nurse row furrow. Do all three furrows from one side of the module, then go to the other side and do that half using the same technique.

Large seed, sowing by broadcasting
For large-seed crops, generally, rows are by far the best way of sowing. They are orderly, easy to tend to, and easy to harvest.

The exception is peas. To get good production a lot of closely spaced seed is needed. Traditionally they are sown in drills. But, then as they grow, supports are needed and it becomes a lot of work for a small yield. For this reason I choose a dwarf variety and broadcast them. The sowing is easy, a thick stand of vines is obtained, and no supports are needed.

Small seed, sowing by broadcasting
For many years I used to broadcast small seeds such as lettuce, arugula, and endive. But since the development of the triplex row system I no longer have any reason to do so and no small-seed crops are broadcast.

Thinning and general care

No one likes to thin. It is psychologically difficult. The key to minimizing this chore is in the sowing.

Large seed can easily be spaced at the exact distances for mature plants. Similarly, if extra care is taken to sow small seed crops far enough apart so that the sprouts will not be too close together when they come up, little or no thinning is needed until they are large enough to eat.

Caring for the health of your plants necessitates good soil management. Keep the soil from crusting and always maintain an even moisture. One should always keep this very basic rule of thumb uppermost in mind.

Crops planted in single rows

The crops that are planted in single rows can be put into two categories: Tall growers and low growers. Their thinning and general care needs are different.

Tall growing large seed crops: If the seed was spaced at the correct distances in the furrows, little or no thinning will be necessary. Plants should be standing at the proper spacing.

If rows are more than 4 inches apart, to avoid cultivation put down a thin mulch as soon as the seedlings are several inches tall. Soil moisture will be held in and weed growth retarded.

If no mulch is used, cultivation probably will be needed as it is important to keep the soil from compacting. But cultivate only if necessary, and then shallowly. Pull weeds if they get too big.

Low-growing small-seed crops: As the seeds germinate and grow, weeds will also be growing. In the early stages this is beneficial. They will shade the soil, keeping the moisture in and preventing it from crusting. They are in effect "unpaid helpers."

When the seedlings have grown so that they begin to crowd each other, pull every other one and thin the weeds. At this stage they are still useful. Thin the weeds selectively, pull all within rows and any others that are too close to the plants. Let some weeds between the rows stay, as they will keep the soil from drying out.

By the time the plants are ready for the second thinning the weeds will have served their purpose and they can all be pulled.

The above gives an overview as to thinning and general care

45

of tall and low growing crops sown in single rows. Of course, no general instructions can fully cover all crops as their needs vary. Detailed instructions are given on individual crop pages.

Leaf Crops planted in triplex rows
Only small-seed leaf vegetables are sown in triplex rows. The basic method, the cut-and-come-again method, or a combination of both can be used. The type of crop sown and its ultimate use will determine which method is the most suitable.

<u>Basic method:</u> All rows are thinned either two or three times, depending on the final spacing required. The procedure is to pull plants as far as can be reached into the center of the bed, then go around to the other side and pick up from where you left off.

1) Seeds are sown at 1-inch intervals. <u>For this explanation assume that all germinate and come up at that distance apart.</u>

2) When the seedlings have developed at least three true leaves and are big enough for use, retain the first plant at one end of the main row and then pull every other one. This will leave the remaining plants 2 inches apart. After that, further harvesting, as needed, is done only from both of the nurse rows. Follow the same process until all rows stand at that spacing.

3) When plants have grown so that they begin to crowd each other, continue this thinning/harvesting by pulling once more. Do the main row first, pulling every other one, spacing to 4 inches apart. But now, in both nurse rows, harvest by pulling all plants <u>directly opposite</u> those left standing in the main row. This will result in staggered rows giving a little extra space all around them.

For plants such as parsley, whose final spacing is 4 inches, do not pull any more from the main row. As needed, pull only from nurse rows until both are fully harvested.

4) Some plants require an 8-inch spacing. For those, repeat the procedure of pulling every other one. Harvest from the main row first. Pull as needed until the remaining plants are 8 inches apart, then leave to mature.

In the nurse rows do the same. But when additional harvesting is needed keep pulling any of the remaining plants randomly until both nurse rows have been eliminated.

<u>Cut-and-come-again method:</u> This technique relies on the fact that many leaf crops will regrow after being cut, allowing

TRIPLEX ROW; BASIC METHOD

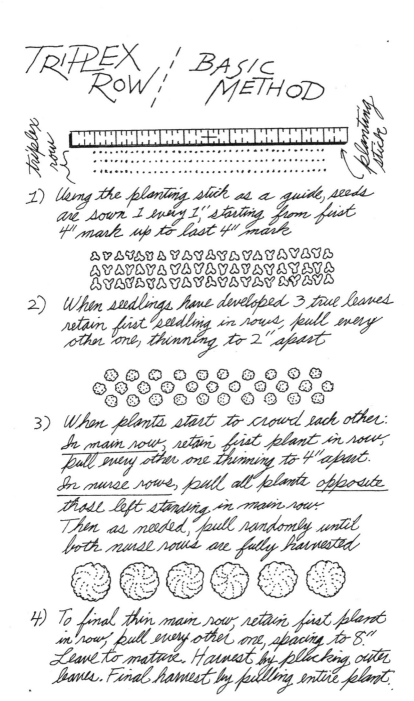

Triplex row

planting stick

1) Using the planting stick as a guide, seeds are sown 1 every 1", starting from first 4" mark up to last 4" mark

2) When seedlings have developed 3 true leaves retain first seedling in rows, pull every other one, thinning to 2" apart

3) When plants start to crowd each other:
In main row, retain first plant in row, pull every other one thinning to 4" apart.
In nurse rows, pull all plants opposite those left standing in main row.
Then as needed, pull randomly until both nurse rows are fully harvested

4) To final thin main row, retain first plant in row, pull every other one, spacing to 8". Leave to mature. Harvest by plucking outer leaves. Final harvest by pulling entire plant.

TRIPLEX ROW; CUT-AND-COME-AGAIN METHOD

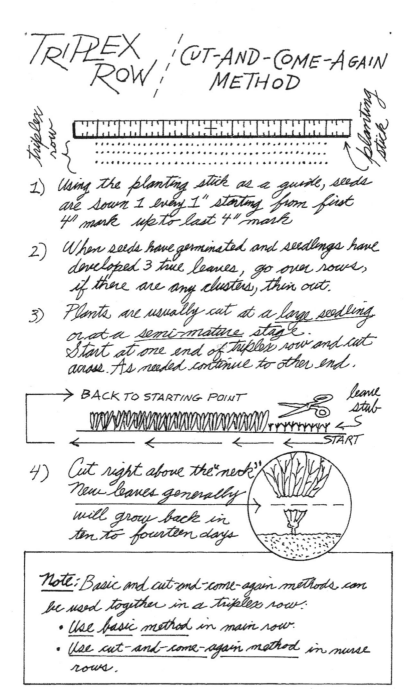

1) Using the planting stick as a guide, seeds are sown 1 every 1" starting from first 4" mark up to last 4" mark

2) When seeds have germinated and seedlings have developed 3 true leaves, go over rows, if there are any clusters, thin out.

3) Plants are usually cut at a _large seedling_ or at a _semi-mature_ stage. Start at one end of triplex row and cut across. As needed continue to other end.

4) Cut right above the "neck". New leaves generally will grow back in ten to fourteen days

Note: Basic and cut-and-come-again methods can be used together in a triplex row:
- Use _basic method_ in main row.
- Use _cut-and-come-again method_ in nurse rows.

them to be harvested over a long period of time without doing any resowing. Hence, thinning is only needed when seedlings are young to establish the initial spacing. All rows are treated the same. The objective is to have an overall even distribution of the individual plants.

As in the basic method seeds are sown at 1-inch intervals. After germination, when the seedlings have developed three true leaves, go over the rows and thin any clumps. At the same time pull any weeds that may have germinated. Usually that will be the only thinning necessary. However, situations at various stages may require some further thinning.

Once seedlings get larger, since all plants are very close together, no cultivation is required. Very few new weed seeds will germinate under these conditions. If any weeds do grow, they will be exposed after every cutting. Just pull them out.

Harvesting is done either at the large seedling stage, when the plants have developed about six true leaves or they can be allowed to grow larger and be cut when semi-mature.

Depending on the size of the plant, cut at about $\frac{1}{2}$–1 inch above their base. New leaves generally will grow back from the stump in 10 to 14 days. By the time you have harvested to the end of the triplex row, usually, the plants first cut will have regrown and be ready for a second harvesting: more often than not a third and sometimes even a fourth cutting can be had.

Note: This cut-and-come-again method can also be combined with the basic method as follows:
1) Basic method is used just in the main row.
2) The cut-and-come-again method is used only in both nurse rows.

Adjusting the theory to reality (the very small seed factor)
In theory if seed is sown in the furrow at 1-inch intervals, when the seedlings come up they should be spaced 1-inch apart.

The reality is, with very small seed such as lettuce, endive, arugula, and parsley, they can move very easily. Rain, normal watering, and other causes can make them shift. Also some will not germinate. As a result, upon germination, invariably there will be clumps and gaps here and there.

Thin out these clumps in all rows right away so that the

remaining seedlings are more or less equal distance apart. Gaps, if extreme, can be filled in with thinnings.

Therefore it is not always simply a matter of pulling every other one as described previously, because spacing will vary. It is really a matter of using good judgment to determine which seedlings to pull to approximate the even spacing that you want.
Fill in any excessive gaps in the main row by transplanting seedlings from the nurse rows.

As for the nurse rows, ordinarily, it is not worth the bother to fill in any gaps since the plants will be harvested young.

Crops that were sown by broadcasting
Peas are the only vegetable sown by broadcasting in the modular garden, having been deliberately sown thickly so as to result in close growing plants; no thinning is done. Neither is any cultivating or staking. The dwarf plants will support each other and shade the soil, choking out most weeds.

Cultivation and mulching
The ideal soil is light, open, and fine on the surface, well drained, rough, and alive below. In nature, soils are opened up by fungi, by earthworms, by roots, and by dead plants that contribute organic matter. This type of soil is very fertile.

After a new garden has been double dug, has good drainage, and is in good tilth, its structure should be disturbed as little as possible. The under the surface life will return to normal and should be allowed to continue uninterrupted. There should not be any annual digging up of the beds.

The cover of close-growing plants will create a mini-climate under their leaves, a "living mulch" protecting the soil and keeping it open. This living mulch and organic mulches are two of nature's ways of protecting the soil and keeping it open: excellent soil management techniques.

Nevertheless, now and then, there is still a need for the time honored tradition of cultivating with hand tools to control weeds and to keep the soil open.

Good soil management starts at the end of a growing season in the fall. To reduce the possibility of the carry over of disease and garden pests from one year to the next, after the crops have been fully harvested, the beds are stripped bare. They are then given an overall shallow cultivation with a rake to expose any left behind bugs or their eggs. The plots are left fallow for several weeks, then, after a light raking to uproot any weeds that may have sprouted, they are mulched with a 3- to 4-inch layer of shredded leaves. (A quick way to shred leaves is to run them over with a rotary lawn mower.) This mulch will insulate the soil, allowing the under the surface life to continue through the cold winter months.

About two or three weeks before the date of the first spring planting, the mulch is removed. The beds are then given a shallow cultivation with the rake to kill any overwintered larvae and left bare. On the planting date, a light raking is given to uproot any weed sprouts and to smooth out. For the sowing of large seed that is all that is necessary; for small seed the soil may have to be made a little finer. But don't make it too fine or it will turn into mud when it gets wet, plus in the sun it will bake into a concrete like surface. If rubbed between your hands soil should crumble into small pieces. You don't want it to be like a powder.

Once the seeds have germinated and are up, cultivation should be practiced only when there is a very good reason to do so. Overuse of the cultivating tool increases the risk of pest and disease attack, as well as causing more weeds to grow. Dormant weed seeds remain viable for years. The more the soil is cultivated, the more weed seeds will be brought to the surface and germinate. Undisturbed soil keeps the weed seeds under the surface and dormant. Use mulches as much as possible.

For leaf plants sown in triplex rows, there usually is little or no need for cultivation. The close spacing of the seedlings along with any weeds that grow create the "living mulch" effect. In the first thinning of the seedlings, weeds should be pulled selectively so as not to leave too much bare ground. But be sure to pull any pernicious weeds such as quackgrass. At the second thinning, as you thin, pull all weeds.

Once the nurse row plants have been fully harvested and the main row stands alone, occasionally, a little shallow cultivating with a hand cultivator may be necessary. When the main row plants have grown so that the tops touch each other, shading the ground underneath, no further cultivation should be necessary

51

as very few weeds will grow in shaded soil.

For large plants sown in 8-inch spaced single rows, since the spaces between rows are greater than the shadows of the young seedlings, there will be no "living mulch" effect. Therefore to avoid the need for cultivation an actual mulch will have to be put down. As soon as the seedlings are up and growing well, pull any weeds and spread a thin shredded leaf mulch between rows and around the plants. This will hold soil moisture in and retard any further weed growth.

If a mulch is not used, cultivation probably will be needed. If the soil begins to crust, open it up using the hand cultivator. Use the tip of a tine to work around the plants, being careful not to harm them by going too deep. In between rows use the full head to break up the surface: Hill up slightly around the base of stems to smother any weeds and to give more support. Do not cultivate any more than necessary. Whenever possible, pull weeds.

For widely spaced plants, such as tomatoes, cultivation is the only practical method to control weeds and prevent crusting in the early stages of their growth. Use the hand cultivator. Cultivate shallowly, keeping the soil loose and friable. Hill up a little around the base of the plant stems.

When the soil has been thoroughly warmed, remove all weeds, lightly cultivate, water thoroughly, and mulch with shredded leaves. This mulch will prevent the soil from drying out in hot weather, maintaining an even soil moisture, and also help control blight.

Some vegetables grown in the garden are intercropped. Their treatment is discussed as encountered.

Transplanting
There will be times when transplanting a seedling from one spot to another is necessary, usually to fill a gap after a thinning. Whatever the reason, it must be done carefully to be successful.

Do not attempt to transplant until the plant has produced four true leaves or more. Avoid transplanting on a hot windy day. Choose a cloudy, misty, or drizzling day. If this is not possible, transplant in the late afternoon after the sun has started to go down and has lost most of its heat.

The soil at the new site should be moist. If it is necessary to add water to the soil, do it a day ahead of time. Dig a hole about 6 inches deep. The seedling should be watered thoroughly a day ahead of time. Do not disturb the seedling's roots any more than necessary. Take up as much surrounding soil as possible with it. Set it at the same depth as it was before. Firm the soil around the stem with your fingers. Leave a slight depression to hold water. Then pour about a pint of water around the base of the plant. Shade with a cardboard "tent" for a few days (to make a tent, fold a strip of cardboard in half to form a capital "A").

Watering
It is especially important to be aware of soil structure when watering. Remember that plant roots grow in the air spaces between the soil particles. Water will fill the air spaces pushing out the air. As the water drains, air is pulled back in, replenishing the roots with oxygen.

When submerged in water, plant roots will stop growing. A waterlogged soil will interrupt growth, resulting in irreversible harm. On the other hand, too little water will also interrupt growth. This is known as water stress. If this happens, the plant will think it is dying and tries to rush to seed.

It is of utmost importance to avoid either of these extremes. Strive to maintain an even moisture level in the soil.

That being the case it is obvious that the main factor in determining how much water a garden needs is the makeup of its soil. Water will go right through a sandy soil, leaving precious little behind for the plant to drink. There will be no reservoir for the roots to draw needed moisture, and very quickly the plants will need another watering. On the other hand, a soil that has a high organic content will hold the moisture and watering will have to be done less frequently. In fact, there could be periods when no watering at all is necessary.

A good soil improvement program is key to your watering program. This cannot be stressed enough. Make it a consistent routine to spread a layer of compost over the soil surface before every planting. Over the years this simple act will slowly build up the moisture holding capacity of the soil.

Regardless of what type of soil is in the garden, it must always be kept firmly in mind that the root of a plant is what needs to get the water. On newly sprouted seedlings it is impractical to water each individual one at the root. An overall fine spraying of the entire plot is the only realistic thing to do. But once beyond that stage, overall spraying of the foliage is not only wasteful of water but in many cases harmful.

An effective watering program is one that maintains an even soil moisture throughout the life of the plant. There must always be enough water to satisfy the needs of the root system, but not so much that oxygen is denied to those roots. Too dry and the plants will start dying, too wet and the roots will start to rot.

Soil fills with water from the top down; it also loses water from the top down. You can get a good idea of the moisture content just by looking at its color. Dry soil is lighter in color that moist soil. Paleness is an indication that water is needed.

For watering to be effective the soil must be open and loose so that it will absorb water readily. Crusted soil will not take the water; it will puddle up and run off. If the soil is crusted, cultivate to open it up before watering.

The watering needs of plants will vary according to what stage of growth they are in. As previously mentioned, soil structure also plays a big part in how frequently they need to be watered: some soils hold water better than others. Generally, the higher the organic content of a soil, the more water it will hold. For the efficient watering of the modular garden two watering devices are used: An impulse sprinkler and a watering wand. Each is best suited for a particular purpose.

The impulse sprinkler is used for newly seeded plots. It produces a fine mist that really saturates the soil without washing it away or disturbing the seed. Furthermore, the fine mist will not compact the soil, preventing crusting. It can be set to cover small or large areas. It is used until the seedlings have grown to the point where their roots are well fixed in the soil.

The watering wand is used after the plants have become deep rooted. At this stage the plants should no longer be watered from above, they should be watered at the roots only. With the watering wand this can be accomplished very effectively as the water can be placed precisely where it is wanted.

Again, remember, to water efficiently; make sure that it is the plant's roots that get the water.

Note: In this chapter watering instructions are given describing procedures using a hose, impulse sprinkler, and watering wand. If facilities for their use are not available, a watering can will serve the same purpose. When directions are given for a spray, use the watering can with the sprinkler head on. When a stream is called for, take off the head and let the water run out of the spout and <u>around</u> the plant unimpeded. But control it so as to flow slowly—no surging or flooding.

For the watering of freshly seeded areas ignore length of time given for watering with the impulse sprinkler, just wet down using the can with the sprinkler head attached until soil is well moistened. If rainwater is available use that.

Watering newly seeded plots
Use the impulse sprinkler. The soil must be kept moist during the time the seeds are germinating. If new seeds dry out, they will not germinate. If newly emerging seedlings, lacking the root system to go deep for moisture, dry out, they die. Never forget this. Water is the most important element in the young seedlings' life. If the seed row dries out even just once before the seedlings are well rooted, they will not survive.

Water early in the morning: Water should be absorbed into the soil quickly; it should not take longer than about ten seconds for the shiny layer of water on the surface to disappear. If it starts to take longer that is an indication that the soil has been watered enough. Depending on the soil, the average watering time for a newly seeded plot should be about 15 to 30 minutes. Go out in the late afternoon and check the soil. If the surface has dried out it must be watered again following the same guidelines as were used for the morning watering.

Until plants are well established this regimen should be followed daily: Always water young sprouts early in the morning before the sun gets too hot. If a second watering is needed, try to do it giving enough time for the seedlings to dry before nightfall: wet plants are susceptible to fungal diseases at night.

In the initial planting in the spring, when a crop has been sown in all three modules, the impulse sprinkler can be set to cover all. In other cases it can be set to water only one or two.

Watering established plants

Once the plants are well established they should no longer be watered from above. You should water the soil around the roots only, not the plant. At this stage use the watering wand. With the wand, water can be placed right at the base of the plant and very little is lost to evaporation.

Established plants should not be watered in the morning. Water on leaves when the sun is hot can magnify its rays and put them in danger of sun scorch. It also wastes water through evaporation. In the case of lettuce, water evaporating in the heat could cause a shock, making them liable to bolt.

Use the watering wand by holding its head facing up at ground level; adjust the water flow so that it comes out as a slow stream, not a spray. Let the water flow down in between the rows and around the plants. Adjust the volume of water to suit the crop. Adjust to little more than a trickle for shallow-rooted crops like lettuce and onions, to a greater volume for deep-rooted plants such as tomatoes.

For plants sown by broadcasting, move the wand along all sides until the soil has absorbed enough water.

The water should be absorbed into the soil almost as fast as it comes out of the wand. Don't flood the surface, creating puddles. When the water starts to remain on the surface longer than about 10 seconds, and the soil has reached its capacity, stop. You want to water enough so that the water joins up with the moisture that's already in the soil. There should be a good continuous amount of moisture going right down into the subsoil. But, you don't want to give it so much water that it becomes waterlogged.

This watering should be done late in the afternoon when the sun has declined, approximately two hours before sunset. This cuts down evaporation and, since the sun has lost its heat, if a few drops get on the leaves, no damage will be done. The next day poke a forefinger into the soil. It should be moist for the full length of the finger. If the soil is dry for part or all of that depth, you need to water more.

A consistent soil moisture is paramount. You don't want to keep going from dry to wet, wet to dry, over and over. A plant does best when it is not subjected to these extremes. For that reason use mulches whenever possible.

IMPULSE SPRINKLER

Sprinkler can be adjusted to water only one or all three modules depending on placement and adjustment ⟶

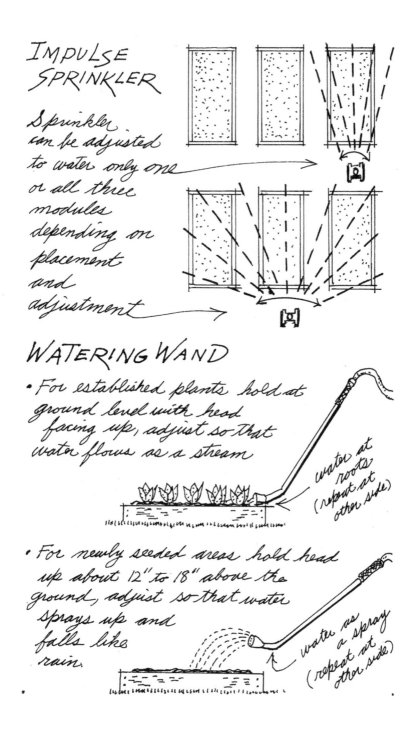

WATERING WAND

• For established plants hold at ground level with head facing up, adjust so that water flows as a stream

water at roots (repeat at other side)

• For newly seeded areas hold head up about 12" to 18" above the ground, adjust so that water sprays up and falls like rain.

water as a spray (repeat at other side)

Watering transplants

Tomatoes and broccoli are put out as transplants. Immediately after setting them in, pour about a quart of water around each tomato plant, about a pint around broccoli.

Then, using the watering wand, water daily late in the afternoon at the root only.

Other transplants, such as those taken from a nurse row to fill in a main row gap, once set and watered at the roots, will receive the same watering treatment as the others of its kind.

Special watering situations

Although the impulse sprinkler is preferred for new sowings, in the succession plantings this is not always possible. In many cases a freshly seeded area will be next to large established crops. In a situation like this it is impossible to adjust the impulse sprinkler to precisely water just that area without wetting the foliage of the adjacent plants.

When this occurs, for practical purposes, a change of routine is called for. In these situations water both at the same time with the watering wand.

Late in the afternoon, as usual, water the established plants at the roots with the water flowing as a gentle stream. Then move over to the freshly seeded area, adjust the flow to a spray, and raise the head of the wand, facing up, about 12 to 18 inches above the ground. The water spray then arcs upward before gently falling down, like rain, on the soil.

This is done until the seeds germinate and the seedlings have become well established.

From that point on, they are treated as the mature crops. Water all at ground level with the water flowing as a slow stream.

Harvesting

Since different crops require different methods of harvesting, no one set of general rules can apply to all.

There are, however, some common factors. Most vegetables are at their prime when young; as they grow older their quality deteriorates. The best time to pick them is right before you are going to use them or store them. Do not let them sit around for any length of time.

General harvesting guidelines for several crop groups are given starting below.

Harvesting legumes
Pods should be harvested young when they are still fairly smooth. The seeds in the pods should be just visible. This is when they are at their peak. If left to fully mature they will lose flavor and tenderness. Also, the plant sensing that it has served its purpose in producing mature seed, will stop producing and start to die. Harvest pods while they are young and the plants will continue to produce.

When harvesting, hold the plant with one hand while picking with the other. These plants have shallow roots and can easily be pulled from the ground. Or, pods can be cut off with a scissors.

Harvesting lettuce and similar leaf vegetables
Lettuce can be harvested in a variety of ways. The most common methods are:

1) The entire plant is pulled while very young.

2) Cut-and-come-again. This technique relies on the fact that after being cut, most leaf vegetables will resprout. The plants are cut a little above their base, leaving a stub in the ground.

This gives further cuttings, which allow harvesting over a period of time. The cutting is generally done at the large seedling or semi-mature stage.

3) Outer leaves of plants in the semi-mature and mature stages are plucked (not cut), leaving the center intact. New leaves will grow back.

4) The plant is grown to maturity. At that stage the entire plant is pulled. In some cases, instead of uprooting the plant, it is cut off inside the bottom leaves above the center core. With enough favorable weather remaining in the season a new small head will regrow.

The guidelines given above generally can be applied to most similar leaf vegetables, such as arugula or endive. Modifications are required for some others, such as Swiss chard and parsley.

Harvesting lettuce and similar leaf crops sown in triplex rows
Harvesting triplex rows involves many aspects of the previously

59

described techniques. Depending on the vegetable, harvesting can be accomplished in several ways.

Basic method: Gives a long harvest; starts with young seedlings through semi-mature to fully mature plants.

1) For an early harvest, as soon as plants are large enough to eat, thin by pulling every other one from all rows.

When they have grown and begin to crowd each other, start with main row and again pull every other one. Create staggered rows. For some plants this will be the main row final spacing. If requiring a wider spacing, repeat the process once more.

Once final main row spacing is attained, then, as needed, pull only from nurse rows randomly until they are fully harvested.

2) Plants in the main row, after their final thinning, are harvested by plucking (not cutting) the outer leaves only. Pluck a few from each plant at a time so that no one plant is decimated.

3) Finally, harvest the main row mature plants by pulling or cutting every other one, as they are needed.

Cut-and-come-again method: Plants harvested in this way are cut at the large seedling or semi-mature stage. Usually when seedlings have developed six true leaves they can be harvested. For some crops it is better to cut them at the semi-mature stage. Trial and error will determine which is appropriate.

Harvesting is done by cutting at a point about $\frac{1}{2}$ to 1 inch above base of plant. Start at one end of the triplex row and cut straight across. Continue down the row, as needed, to the other end. By that time the first cut plants may have regrown from the stumps and are ready for a second cutting. It is possible to get a third and even a fourth cutting: This method is best for mesclun.

Harvesting root crops

Harvest while young; if left to mature they will become woody. Simply pull them from the ground by hand. If harvesting is delayed and the roots have grown too large to be easily pulled by hand, push the blade of a hand trowel down next to the root and lever back and forth, loosening the soil, then pull.

Summation

The preceding are generalizations. For harvesting any crop not covered, as well as those covered, individual instructions are given in chapters 5 and 7. Refer to the pages on each specific vegetable grown for more explicit directions.

Composting

Compost is the finest and most valuable soil conditioner available, and the best part of it is, all of the ingredients needed for its creation can be had for free. It will cost you nothing. Once a pile of organic material is built, it will practically make itself. This happens all the time in nature with no help from anyone.

Don't be put off by "experts" who cite complicated formulas and procedures. They would have you believe that one needs a master's degree in science before attempting such a challenge.

Also to be ignored are ads peddling a wide range of "must have" products, yeasts, bioactivators, and other special compost pile additives. Regular garden soil and anything you add to the pile is already covered with more than enough bacteria to do the job. Worms are another item heavily hyped. Don't buy them! If you build a pile, local earthworms will come.

Organic material over time will rot. The building of a pile is really just a matter of creating the conditions that will speed up the decaying process. Which brings us to the next consideration: what form should the pile take?

Organic material can simply be piled up on the soil in an uncontained pile, a pit can be dug and filled with the material, or the pile can be enclosed in some sort of container.

An open pile is messy, unsightly, and may attract pests. If none of that bothers you, it is a simple, no-cost way to go.

A pit works well and with a lid is practically invisible. Its biggest drawback is that it takes a lot of work to remove the finished compost.

A container is neat, efficient, easy to add to, and easy to remove the finished compost. It is the method recommended.

Compost containers

The New Zealand Box is the grandfather of all of today's compost containers. It is made of wood, 4 feet wide by 4 feet deep by 3 feet high. It has no bottom or top. Boards are nailed to uprights, leaving a $\frac{1}{2}$-inch space between each, to form three sides. The front boards are removable. This is accomplished by leaving a small space between two uprights at the front, creating a channel. The boards are then just slid in and out of this channel. The New Zealand Box is attractive, practical, and efficient. (See illustration on page 65.) If used lumber or discarded wood pallets are available, it can be built very cheaply or even at no cost.

Round containers can be made at low cost by taking a length of wire fencing about 3 feet wide by 9 feet long, bending it into a circle and tying the ends together.

Three sided containers can be made by stacking used bricks or cement blocks, dry, to build the walls. The bricks need to be staggered leaving air gaps between; the concrete blocks are placed on their sides so that the holes provide ventilation.

There are, of course, many other materials and methods of making suitable containers. If you don't care to build one yourself, commercially manufactured bins can be purchased. They come in a wide array of models, are attractive, efficient, and durable. They are, however, also expensive.

Location of the compost pile
The compost pile should be sited in an easily accessible spot on level ground. It should be convenient to you, preferably near a water source.

And of course it should not be too far away from your garden. It should have space all around for good air circulation. It can be in the sun or shade. In the sun it will heat up faster, in shaded spots it will be less likely to dry out.

Building the pile with greens and browns
There are many ways to build a compost pile. I use the simplest way. This method uses materials that are available to any gardener: greens and browns.

Greens (nitrogen rich, wet) are fresh leaves, prunings, green grass, weeds, flowers, plants, garden and kitchen wastes such as vegetable trimmings, banana skins, coffee grounds, tea bags, citrus rinds, melon rinds, carrot tops, fruit skins, etc.

Browns (carbon rich, dry) are fall leaves, dried plants, very small twigs, straw or hay, egg shells, wood chips, or sawdust.

Building the pile is simply a matter of mixing approximately equal amounts of greens and browns.

Materials to avoid—read carefully
For the health of the compost pile, as well as for the overall garden health, don't add any pesticide-treated or diseased plants to the compost pile. (This includes treated or chemically fertilized grass clippings.) Other forbidden materials are pressure-treated wood chips or sawdust, charcoal briquets or their ashes, and obviously, no poison sumac or poison ivy.

As for household wastes, leave out of the collection pail any meats, fats, bones, oils, and all dairy-related products. It is also important that dog, cat, or other carnivorous pet fecal waste never be used. This could expose you and your family to disease when using the compost. When in doubt, leave it out!

Active or passive composting
One can be active, passive, or a little in between when it comes to composting. Active will produce compost quicker, passive later. Active requires regular turning or aerating of the pile. Turning consists of blending fresh ingredients with older material usually using a pitchfork. Aerating is creating vertical air passages in the pile, using an aerating tool, or an old broomstick.

Active: If one has enough greens and browns in roughly equal amounts on hand to build a pile 3 feet square all at once, chops everything into little pieces, keeps the moisture content right, turns or aerates the pile every three to seven days, compost can be produced very quickly, in about three months.

Passive: Using the passive method, one builds the pile as materials become available and lets nature takes its course. With this method it will take much longer to produce compost, at least a year. The time can be shortened if the pile is aerated every time it has shrunk noticeably in size.

I use the passive method, aerating when necessary.

Building a passive compost pile
A little advanced planning is needed when a pile is to be built. Greens are abundant in spring and summer, but browns are not abundant until fall. It therefore requires stockpiling browns in the fall so that they are available for the coming winter plus next season's spring and summer. Collect leaves, put them in large plastic bags, and store in an inconspicuous spot. If, before

sealing, a little garden soil is thrown into the bags and the leaves lightly sprayed with water, it will hasten their breakdown.

In fact, fall is a good time to start a pile since both greens and browns are available at that time. Of course, during the winter months the only greens to be had will be kitchen scraps, but that will be enough. A pile consisting solely of fall leaves and kitchen scraps will make a very fine compost.

To start a pile: First, put down about a 6-inch layer of coarse browns. Then, throw and mix in an equal amount of greens, a sprinkling of soil and wet lightly.

After this initial base has been put down, add and mix in greens and browns in approximately equal amounts as they become available. The pile should be kept moist. If it is consistently too dry, add proportionally more greens than browns; if it is consistently too wet add more browns than greens.

It will take a little time before you get the right proportions. But, in passive composting you don't have to be too concerned about being very precise. No matter what you do, in the end you will have compost.

A covering on the bin will help keep moisture in. If your bin has no lid, a piece of plastic will do. If the pile is dry and rain is forecast, take the covering off and let nature add the needed moisture. Aerate whenever the pile has shrunk noticeably.

Continue adding and mixing greens and browns until the bin is full. It is important that kitchen wastes always be covered. If left uncovered they may attract unwanted pests and cause odors. As soon as they are added, cover immediately with browns.

When one pile is completed, leave it to mature and start another. Three piles are ideal. One being built in the current year, one that was built the previous year and is maturing, and one that was built two years ago and is now finished compost.

Screens

For some sowings of very small seed vegetables I spread a thin layer of fine compost over their seedbed. This fine compost is obtained by sifting through a $\frac{1}{8}$-inch screen. Screens can be bought or you can make your own by stretching a piece of hardware cloth over a wooden frame. Screens of $\frac{1}{4}$ or $\frac{1}{2}$ inch are the most used, as a little coarser compost will usually do just fine.

BUILDING A PASSIVE COMPOST PILE

⑤ In winter
kitchen wastes are
the only greens
available, when adding
cover with browns
immediately!

④ Keep adding and
mixing greens and
browns in roughly
equal amounts
(keep moist)

③ Add and
mix in
an equal
amount
of greens
sprinkle in
a little soil,
moisten
lightly

① In the
fall
stockpile
leaves
(browns)

note:
Cut large material
into smaller pieces
before adding

② Build
the pile
by putting down
a base of browns

THE NEW ZEALAND BOX

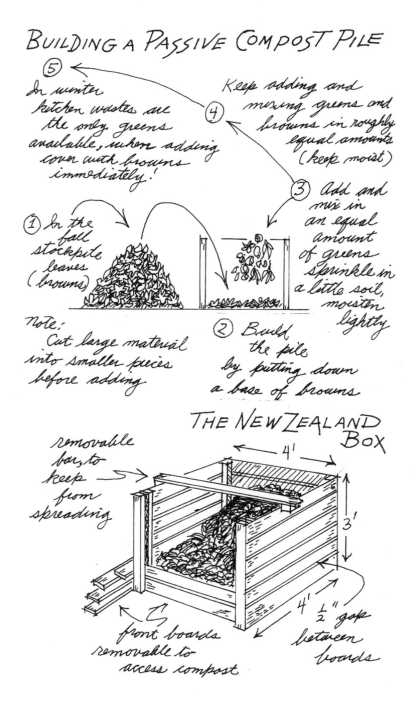

removable
bar, to
keep
from
spreading

4'

3'

4'   ½" gap
      between
      boards

front boards
removable to
access compost

4

Putting it all together

Up to this point the development and various other aspects of the modular system have been discussed individually. Now all of these diverse elements have to be implemented at the appropriate time to bring into being a healthy, productive garden.

It all starts with a garden map. It is an indispensable tool in any gardening system, especially so in the three-module vegetable garden. It shows the crops to be planted, their location, row spacing, planting unit measurements, and planting dates.

The three module vegetable garden map is shown and explained on pages 68 and 69.

In this system the vegetables are grouped into three crop groups: A group, B group, and C group. Each of the crop groups occupies a full module and each group consists of two plantings a season: An initial planting followed by a succession planting. The initial planting is done in three stages. The succession planting is done in four stages.

As the crops of the initial planting become fully harvested, their areas are then cleared and planted with succession crops.

There are, however, several exceptions to this sequence. Swiss chard, parsley, and onions stand for the full season. Furthermore, the Swiss chard and parsley, sown every spring, being hardy biennials, are left to overwinter. With the help of a mulch they usually come through just fine, renewing their growth in the following spring, and are harvested until the new spring sowings are of harvest size, then pulled.

As shown on the garden map, each crop group fills the exact same size space (one full module) and they are interchangeable with each other. Crop rotation is simplified. The map shows the crop groups as they would be located at the start of a new garden. In subsequent years each crop group is rotated, in turn, into a different module. After the initial season the crop group in the first module is planted in the third module and the other two groups move over one. This procedure is fully described in the chapter on crop rotation later in the book.

Vegetables to be planted
The wide range of vegetables grown was selected for many different reasons. Some were chosen because they give the greatest yield for space and effort, others because they grow best either in cool or warm weather. The overall consideration being, that in combination with each other, they will give a continuous harvest from spring into late fall.

The vegetables, their recommended varieties, and amount of seed needed for a season are listed below:

Veg., Variety & Quantity	*Veg., Variety & Quantity*
Arugula *(herb)*	Peas
Astro, 1 pkt.	Improved Laxtons Progress,
Beets	8 ozs.
Detroit Dark Red, 1 pkt.	Onions
Broccoli	Southport White Globe, 1 pkt.
De Cicco, 1 pkt.	Radishes
Bush Beans	Champion, 1 pkt.
Bush Blue Lake, 8 ozs.	Comet, 1 pkt.
Carrots	Swiss Chard
Royal Chantenay, 1 pkt.	Rhubarb Chard, 1 pkt.
Endive	Tomatoes *
Green Curled, 1 pkt.	Delicious, 1 pkt.
Fava Beans	Earliana, 1 pkt.
Aquadulce, 6 ozs.	
Garlic *(herb)*	* *If not growing your*
Elephant, 23 cloves	*own transplants,*
Lettuce	*you will have to buy*
Buttercrunch, 1 pkt.	*whatever is*
Simpson Elite, 1 pkt.	*available at your*
Parsley *(herb)*	*local garden center*
Plain Dark Green Italian, 1 pkt.	*or nursery.*

The Garden Map

This map is an overview of all crops grown.
- *Top row indicates the initial planting.*
- *Bottom row indicates the succession planting.*

The vegetables are grouped into three groups, A group, B group, and C group.

Each year there are two plantings in each module. An initial planting followed by a succession planting.

On the map the top row shows the three modules as sown in the initial planting.

The bottom row shows the same three modules as planted with the succession crops.

In each diagram, all specifics needed are given: names of vegetables, planting dates, row spacing, and other dimensions.

Note: Very Important!

In the individual vegetable instructions that are given in chapters 5 & 7 exact spacing distances between plants are specified for thinning and harvesting.

These are ideals, really not 100% possible in the real world as seed will shift, some will not germinate, and others will come up in clumps.

Use as guidelines only!

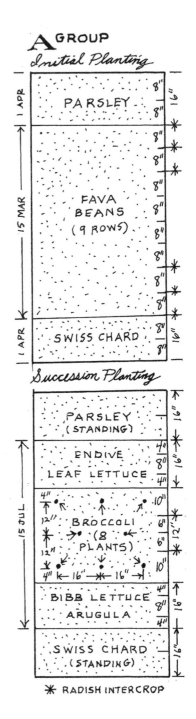

68

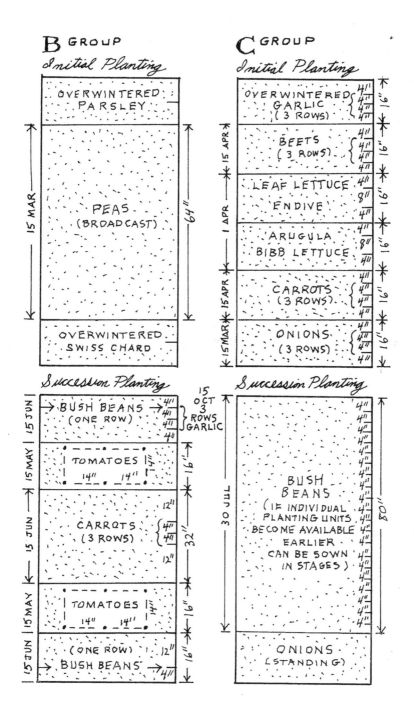

B GROUP
Initial Planting

OVERWINTERED PARSLEY

PEAS (BROADCAST)

64"

15 MAR

OVERWINTERED SWISS CHARD

C GROUP
Initial Planting

OVERWINTERED GARLIC (3 ROWS) — 4" 4" 4" 4" — 16"

BEETS (3 ROWS) — 4" 4" 4" 4" — 16"

LEAF LETTUCE 4" / ENDIVE 8" / 4" — 16"

ARUGULA 4" / BIBB LETTUCE 8" / 4" — 16"

CARROTS (3 ROWS) — 4" 4" 4" — 16"

ONIONS (3 ROWS) — 4" 4" 4" — 16"

15 APR / 1 APR / 15 APR / 15 MAR

Succession Planting

BUSH BEANS (ONE ROW) — 4" 4" 4" 4"

TOMATOES 1½ — 14" 14"

CARROTS (3 ROWS) — 4" 4" / 12"

TOMATOES 1½ — 14" 14"

(ONE ROW) BUSH BEANS — 12" 4"

15 JUN | 15 JUN / 15 MAY / 15 JUN / 15 MAY / 15 JUN

15 OCT 3 ROWS GARLIC

16" / 32" / 16" / 16" / 16"

Succession Planting

4" (repeated rows)

BUSH BEANS (IF INDIVIDUAL PLANTING UNITS BECOME AVAILABLE EARLIER CAN BE SOWN IN STAGES)

80"

30 JUL

ONIONS (STANDING)

69

5

The initial planting

In the established garden the first order of business at the start of each new season is to remove the shredded leaf mulch that was applied in the previous fall. After that the soil must be prepared for the initial planting.

Preparing the beds
About two or three weeks before the earliest spring planting date, remove all of the mulch from the modules, except that covering the overwintering Swiss chard, parsley, and garlic. Pull any endive, arugula, and carrots that have survived the winter.

After the mulch has been removed go over the cleared areas with a rake giving a shallow cultivation to kill any larvae that may have overwintered. Then level off. Leave the soil bare until it is time to plant. At planting time rake the soil lightly to smooth out and to mix the drier surface soil with the moist soil underneath. For large seed sowings that is all that is necessary. For small seed sowings a finer seedbed is needed to ensure good contact with the seed. Go over the area again, smoothing and fining. Then spread a thin layer of fine compost.

As for the overwintering Swiss chard, parsley, and garlic, the mulch covering them must be removed slowly to avoid shocking the plants. Gradually remove it a little at a time until it is completely removed over a period of about four to six weeks, depending on the weather. By that time the plants will have become acclimatized and will resume their growth.

GETTING STARTED

PREPARING THE MODULES FOR THE NEW SEASON

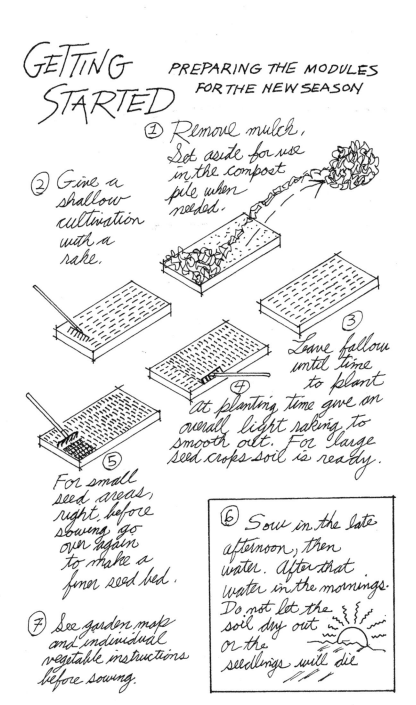

① Remove mulch. Set aside for use in the compost pile when needed.

② Give a shallow cultivation with a rake.

③ Leave fallow until time to plant

④ At planting time give an overall light raking to smooth out. For large seed crops soil is ready.

⑤ For small seed areas, right before sowing go over again to make a finer seed bed.

⑥ Sow in the late afternoon, then water. After that water in the mornings. Do not let the soil dry out or the seedlings will die

⑦ See garden map and individual vegetable instructions before sowing.

Initial planting schedule

The initial planting is one of cool weather hardy and semi-hardy vegetables. They can withstand a little frost and the earlier that they can go in, the earlier the harvest. The initial planting is done in three stages. It starts as soon as the soil can be worked with the sowing of the hardiest followed by sowings in approximately two week intervals of the semi-hardiest.

First sowing (about March 15th):
    A group Fava Beans
    A group Radishes (intercropped within fava bean rows)
    B group Peas
    C group Onions

Second sowing (about April 1st):
    A group Parsley, with Radishes as row markers
    A group Swiss Chard
    B group Tomato Transplants—sow indoors
    C group Leaf Lettuce
    C group Endive
    C group Arugula
    C group Bibb Lettuce

Third sowing (about April 15th):
    C group Beets
    C group Carrots

Sow in the afternoon. After sowing, water using the impulse sprinkler. Position and adjust it so that the range of travel will cover all of the newly seeded modules. If water stays on the surface longer than the time it takes to slowly count from 1,001 to 1,010 (10 seconds), stop! You have watered enough.

Early the next morning water again. Check the soil in the afternoon. If surface has dried out, rewater. Soil must be kept moist for the seed to germinate and for the seedlings to thrive. Do not let the soil dry out. This early morning watering regimen must be followed until plants are well established. Then water late in the afternoon at the roots.

Overwintered plants and the previous fall garlic planting

Before getting into the details of the initial planting; a few words about the crops that are already in the garden. Swiss chard and parsley, being biennials, are specifically overwintered so that they can be the source of supply in the following season until the new sowing of these vegetables reach harvest size. Any endive, arugula, or carrots that may have overwintered should be pulled immediately as an early harvest. Their spaces are needed for new crops. The overwintered garlic, once the mulch has been removed, is treated as an emerging newly planted crop.

Parsley

In the second year parsley will tend to bolt quickly. It throws up a seed stalk when it's about a year old. But by pinching off the tops of the seed stalks you can prolong the season of leaf yield. If managed carefully, keeping the seed stalks closely cut, the plants should be harvestable up until thinnings from the newly sown crop can start filling your needs.

Swiss chard

The Swiss chard will also tend to bolt quickly the second year. However, with careful management the overwintered plants will be able to supply early greens until the current crop reaches harvest size. A very versatile vegetable, the younger leaves can be used in salads, mature leaves cooked as spinach, and the stalks used raw as celery or cooked as asparagus. While the older leaves are harvested from the outer portions of the plant, new leaves are being formed at the center. This makes it possible to harvest greens repeatedly: one of the few plants to provide a continuous harvest without successive plantings.

Garlic

Having been sown the previous October for summer harvest in the current season, aside from removing its mulch, there is little to do. Start by removing the mulch slowly, a little at a time. As the weather warms, gradually remove more. Finally, leave a thin layer on the soil. See page 117 in chapter 7 for care instructions.

In this chapter, as reference guides, each vegetable grown is listed with a description of the recommended variety and guidelines as to planting, general care, and harvesting.

Initial planting, A group

Fava Beans

Aquadulce (recommended variety)
Vigorous, very hardy: Upright plants grow to a height of 24 inches. Large pods contain 7 or 8 greenish white seeds.
65 days to maturity.
Large seed.

How to plant
Plant in 9 single staggered rows, 8 inches apart.
Make ¼-inch-deep furrows and space seeds 6 inches apart.
Intercrop radishes within the first three and last three rows.
In rows where radishes are to be intercropped, midway between the beans, space 2 radish seeds equidistant.
When all fava bean seeds have been placed in the furrow, with a forefinger push them into the soil about 1½ inches.
For radish seed, simply firm, ¼ inch is their correct depth.
Cover all furrows with compost, then water.

General care
No thinning needed. Once plants are up and are a few inches tall, put down a thin shredded leaf mulch around plants and between all rows that have not been intercropped with radishes. Mulch those spaces after the radishes have been harvested. The mulch will hold the soil moisture in. Water established plants at the roots only. If you don't mulch, cultivation may be necessary. These plants have shallow roots, if you do cultivate, hill up about 2 to 3 inches around their stems to give support.

Harvesting
Pull radishes as needed. Beans are ready to pick 65 to 90 days after planting. Pick when pods are almost fully grown but not yet ripe. Beans will be slightly visible as bumps in the pods. Shell and cook like lima beans. **Caution: Some people are allergic to fava beans. *Take proper precautions before eating.***

Initial planting, A group intercrop

Radishes

Champion (recommended variety)
Vigorous, large tops, bright red round large size: Crisp snow-white flesh. Good for early spring or fall planting.
20 days to maturity.
Small seed.

How to plant
Radishes are a hardy quick growing crop. They are in the ground for such a short time that they are best sown as an intercrop, or together with slow emerging seeds to break the soil crust, and mark the rows. They are harvested before the slower crop needs the space. In the initial planting they are sown as follows:
1) With fava beans as a soil breaker and row marker.
Radishes are intercropped within several rows of fava beans. After the fava beans have been placed in the furrows, two radish seeds are spaced 2 inches apart, midway between the beans. Radish seed is firmed; fava beans are pushed into the soil to a depth of about 1½ inches (See fava bean planting instructions on facing page.)
2) With parsley as a soil breaker and row marker.
Drop 1 seed every 4 inches within all rows. Then push into the soil with your forefinger to a depth of ¼ inch.

General care
Need very little care. They require only one inch around them. Just pull the fastest growing ones for eating. Do not require cultivation. Just keep moist at the root from seedling to harvest.

Harvesting
To harvest simply pull them out of the ground. Best when they are pulled young. If allowed to grow too big they tend to become hot and woody. In Italy, the leaves are used in salads. This is an acquired taste, but try it, you might like it!

Initial planting, B group

Peas

Improved Laxton's Progress (recommended variety)
Extra early: Bush, dwarf vines grow to about 16 inches tall. Dark
green pods are $4\frac{1}{2}$ to $4\frac{3}{4}$ inches long.
55 days to maturity. Large seed.

How to plant
Make a center line lengthwise in the soil, splitting the area to be
planted. Standing at one side of the module, reach a rake across
to the opposite side and pull toward you so as to skim off about
$\frac{1}{2}$ inch of soil, piling it up in a ridge slightly beyond the center
line, in effect making a wide, shallow furrow. Go over to the other
side and broadcast thickly. Holding the rake vertically, tamp down
firmly, pressing the peas into the soil. Lightly rake the soil from
the ridge over the peas to cover. When all peas have been covered,
tamp down again, but this time lighter. Repeat the same procedure
on the other half of the planting area, then water.

General care
No thinning necessary. Plants are dwarfs and do not have to be
staked, they will support each other. Since seeds are sown thickly,
plants will smother any weeds starting to grow. No cultivating
necessary. Once seedlings are established, water at the roots only.

Harvesting
Harvest as soon as pods are filled—young and tender. Pick right
before they're to be eaten, as their sugar starts turning into starch
once off the vine. Plants have shallow roots, when harvesting hold
vine with one hand while picking with the other, otherwise the
plant may be uprooted. (Or cut pods off with a scissors.) Pick the
peas low down on the vines first, those higher up later.
   Note: *The above pea sowing, due to succession planting is
used primarily as a cover crop to improve the soil for the later
planting of tomatoes. Any kind of a harvest is secondary.*

PLANTING PEAS By BROADCASTING

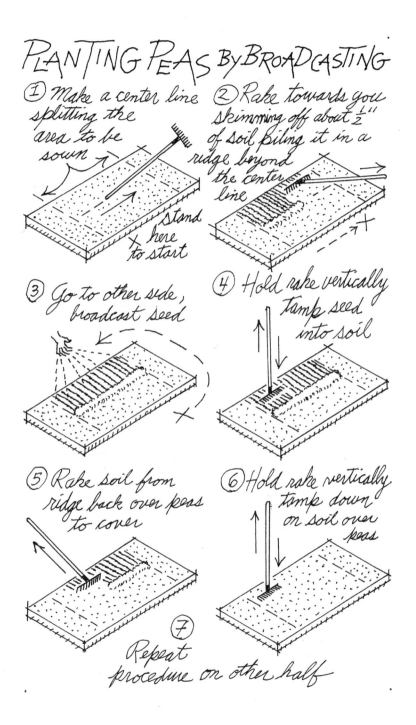

① Make a center line splitting the area to be sown

Stand here to start

② Rake towards you skimming off about ½" of soil piling it in a ridge beyond the center line

③ Go to other side, broadcast seed

④ Hold rake vertically Tamp seed into soil

⑤ Rake soil from ridge back over peas to cover

⑥ Hold rake vertically tamp down on soil over peas

⑦ Repeat procedure on other half

Initial planting, C group

Onions

Southport White Globe (recommended variety)
Can be used as green bunching onions (scallions) and also as a
large white globe onion: Not for storage.
65 days (for scallions), 110–120 days (for mature bulbs).
Small seed.

How to plant
Plant in 3 single conventional rows, 4 inches apart.
Make ½-inch furrows. Sow 1 seed every 1 inch.
Firm with curled forefinger, cover with compost, water.

General care
Rows need to be kept weed free. This is very important as the
small roots need all the nourishment available and weeds will
rob them of essential nutrients. Pull all weeds within the rows to
avoid harming the roots. Being shallow rooted, onions need a lot
of water. Keep the soil open and water frequently. No thinning is
necessary. Generally they are pretty much pest and disease free.

Harvesting
Since onions can be used at any stage, they can be harvested over
a long period of time. Start harvesting as scallions by pulling
every other one. Remaining plants will then stand 2 inches apart.
Repeat the process for subsequent scallion harvesting. This will
result in a distance of 4 inches between remaining plants. At that
spacing they can be left to develop large globes until fully ripe.
You will know that they are ready when the tops begin to wither
and fall over. During a period of dry weather, pull and allow them
to cure by leaving them on top of the ground until thoroughly
dried. This takes about 5 to 10 days. If rain threatens bring them
under cover. After they are cured, cut off tops about 5 inches
above the bulb, braid or just tie the stems together and hang in a
cool dry place until used.

Initial planting, A group

Parsley

Plain Dark Green Italian (recommended variety)
Celery leaf, large flat glossy, deeply cut dark green leaves. Has
much more flavor than curled type.
78 days to maturity.
Small seed.

How to plant
To speed germination, soak seeds in warm water overnight.
Plant in 1 triplex row:
Make ¼-inch furrows, sow 1 seed every 1 inch; do not cover.
    Curl a forefinger and firm. *Go back and drop a radish seed
every 4 inches in rows, with fingertip, push into soil ¼ inch.*
When sowing is completed, water.

General care
Radishes will come up first, they require no thinning; just pull
the biggest ones as they mature. When parsley seedlings come up
and are big enough for use, harvest starting with the main row.
Pull every other one, thinning plants in all rows to 2 inches apart.
When plants begin to crowd each other it is time to final thin: In
main row, space to 4 inches by pulling every other one. Then in
nurse rows, as needed, pull all plants opposite those left standing
in main row. At that point leave the main row, as is, to grow to
maturity and just take from both nurse rows randomly until they
are fully harvested. Pull any weeds in the main row.

Harvesting
Thinnings and the pulling of the nurse row plants supply the early
harvests. When main row plants stand alone, they are harvested
by picking leaves as you need them. Snap off stems at their base.
Pick the outer leaves only; the heart of the plant will grow more.
It will bear better if you pick just a few from each plant at a time
so that no one plant will be decimated.

Initial planting, A group

Swiss Chard

Rhubarb Chard (recommended variety)
Deep green heavily savoyed leaves. Colorful crimson stalks:
Grows well in either cool or hot weather.
55 days to maturity.
Small seed.

How to plant
Plant in 1 triplex row:
Make ¾-inch furrows, sow 1 seed every 1 inch, curl your
    forefinger and firm, then cover with compost, water.

General care
Like beets, each seed ball contains more than one seed. When
seedlings come up, thin any clumps so that only one plant stands
every 1 inch. When they are big enough to use, starting with the
main row, pull every other one, thinning all to 2 inches apart.
Use thinnings in salads. After all plants have been thinned to this
spacing, again starting in the main row, as needed, start pulling to
thin to 4 inches apart. Then in nurse rows pull all plants that are
opposite those left standing in main row. This will give all plants
a little more growing room. Once that phase is done, final thin
main row plants to 8 inches by again pulling every other one. Do
the same in nurse rows. Finish up the early harvest by randomly
pulling from both nurse rows until they are eliminated.

Harvesting
Thinnings and nurse row plants supply the early harvest. After
final thinning, the harvest of main row plants is done by plucking outer leaves. Grasp stem close to rootstock and detach with
a sharp downward tug, or twist. At maturity entire plant can be
harvested leaving only the center heart. The plant will regrow.
Leaves can be added to salads raw or can be cooked like spinach,
stalks are used like celery or cooked as asparagus.

Initial planting, C group

Leaf Lettuce

Simpson Elite (recommended variety)
Light lime green crinkled leaves, mild sweet flavor. An improved
slow bolt strain: Similar to Black-Seeded Simpson.
41 days to maturity.
Small seed.

How to plant
Plant in 1 triplex row, side by side with endive:
Make ¼-inch furrows, sow 1 seed every 1 inch, firm, then water.

General care
When seedlings come up they should be about 1 inch apart. Once
they have developed at least three true leaves and are big enough
to eat, retain the first plant at one end of all rows and pull every
other one. This will space plants to 2 inches apart. Thin and weed
at the same time. Water established plants at roots only.

Harvesting
The first early harvest is achieved by the initial thinning of the
young seedlings. That will be followed by a second harvest when
the plants begin to crowd each other. Pull every other plant from
the main row, spacing to 4 inches, and then pull plants in the
nurse rows directly opposite those left standing in the main row.
Final thin to 8 inches by retaining first plants in all rows and
again pulling every other one. In nurse rows once this is done any
further harvesting is accomplished by pulling plants randomly
until both nurse rows have been eliminated. In the main row, after
final thinning, leave remaining plants to mature. Harvest them by
plucking, not cutting, outer leaves only. New leaves will regrow.
Just pluck a few from each plant at a time so that no one plant is
devastated. At maturity harvest by pulling the entire plant. Pull
alternate plants first so as not to expose too much bare earth to the
sun, then, as needed, pull those remaining.

Initial planting, C group

Endive

Green Curled (recommended variety)
Dark finely cut curled leaves: Slightly bitter taste. Excellent for use in mesclun (mixed greens salads): Disease and insect free. 90 days to maturity. Small seed.

How to plant
Plant in 1 triplex row, side by side with leaf lettuce:
Make ¼-inch furrows, sow 1 seed every 1 inch.
Do not cover seed, it is light sensitive; just firm, then water.

General care
Very little care is required since all will be cut at a young stage. None of the plants will stand to maturity. When seedlings come up they should be about 1 inch apart. Go over the rows, thin any clusters and pull any weeds. Generally no further thinning will be needed, unless severe overcrowding develops. All rows are treated the same. As seedlings get bigger, since they are so close to each other, the soil will be shaded. Very few weeds will sprout under those conditions. Any weeds that do grow will be exposed when plants are cut for use. Just pull them out at that time. Water little and often.

Harvesting
Plants are harvested at the semi-mature stage by the cut-and-come-again method. Endive will resprout after being cut. This allows for an extended harvest without resowing. When the plants have passed beyond the large seedling stage and are semi-mature, start cutting. Begin at one end of the triplex row and cut right across the full width. Cut at a point about 1 inch above the base of the plant. New leaves will grow from the stump in the ground. As needed, continue in this manner to the other end. By that time the plants that were first cut should have regrown. Generally, two or three cuttings can be had from a sowing.

Initial planting, C group

Arugula

Astro (recommended variety)
Dark green wide tongue-shaped leaves. Strong spicy taste gives a peppery flavor to a salad: A very versatile herb. 40 days to maturity. Small Seed.

How to plant
Plant in 1 triplex row, side by side with bibb lettuce: Make ¼-inch furrows. Sow 1 seed every 1 inch, firm, then water.

General care
Very little care is required since all will be cut at a young stage. None of the plants will stand to maturity. When seedlings come up they should be about 1 inch apart. Go over the rows, thin any clusters, and pull any weeds. Generally no further thinning will be needed, unless severe overcrowding develops. All rows are treated the same. As seedlings get bigger, since they are so close to each other, the soil will be shaded. Very few weeds will sprout under those conditions. Any weeds that do grow will be exposed when plants are cut, just pull them out. Water little and often.

Harvesting
Spring sown arugula will mature and bolt to seed very quickly. For that reason, it is not grown to maturity but is harvested at the large seedling stage by the cut-and-come-again method. Arugula will resprout after being cut. This allows for an extended harvest without resowing. When the seedlings have developed six true leaves, it is time to start cutting. Begin at one end of the triplex row and cut right across the full width. Cut at least ½ inch above the base of the plant. New leaves will resprout from the stump in the ground. As needed, continue in this manner to the other end. By that time the plants that were first cut should have regrown. Generally, two or three cuttings, and sometimes more, are possible from a single sowing.

Initial planting, C group

Bibb Lettuce

Buttercrunch (recommended variety)
Medium green; forms a loose head. Long-standing, doesn't get
bitter in heat. Thick crisp leaves.
60 days to maturity.
Small seed.

How to plant
Plant in 1 triplex row, side by side with arugula:
Make ¼-inch furrows, sow 1 seed every 1 inch, firm, then water.

General care
When seedlings come up they should be about 1 inch apart. Once
they have developed at least three true leaves and are big enough
to eat, retain the first plant at one end of all rows and pull every
other one. This will space plants to 2 inches apart. Thin and weed
at the same time. Water established plants at roots only.

Harvesting
The first early harvest is achieved by the initial thinning of the
young seedlings as described above. That will be followed by a
second harvest when the plants begin to crowd each other. Pull
every other plant from the main row, spacing to 4 inches, then
pull plants in the nurse rows <u>directly opposite</u> those left standing
in the main row. Final thin to 8 inches by retaining first plants in
all rows and again pulling every other one. In nurse rows once
this is done, any further harvesting is accomplished by pulling
plants randomly until both nurse rows have been eliminated. In
the main row, after final thinning, leave remaining plants to grow
to maturity. Harvest them by plucking, not cutting, outer leaves
only. New leaves will regrow. Just pluck a few from each plant at
a time so that no one plant is devastated. At maturity harvest by
pulling the entire plant. Pull alternate plants first, then, as needed,
those remaining.

Initial planting, C group

Beets

Detroit Dark Red (recommended variety)
Round, dark red tap root and large leaves: Extremely sweet flavor.
Both leaves and roots can be eaten.
63 days to maturity.
Small seed.

How to plant
Plant in 3 single conventional rows, 4 inches apart:
Make ¾-inch furrows, sow 1 seed every 1 inch.
Curl a forefinger and firm, cover with compost.
When all rows have been completed, water.

General care
Beet seed is actually a ball that contains more than one seed. If
not thinned, clumps of plants will grow rather than individual
plants. As soon as they come up thin all excess plants so that there
are no clumps by pinching off at ground level or cutting them
off with a small pointed scissors. Thin again when the plants are
3 to 4 inches high by pulling every other plant; at the same time
pull any weeds. When the roots are about the size of a marble (a
diameter of about ½ inch), final thin again by pulling every other
plant, then leave them for full growth. All of the thinnings can be
used in salads. They don't really need to be cultivated, just keep
moist at the roots from seedling to harvest. Try to maintain an
even moisture in the soil. Do not soak. If the ground is continually saturated, the root will rot.

Harvesting
Simply pull the beets out of the ground. Wash the earth off, never
scrape or the skin may be damaged, causing loss of flavor. Beets
are best when 1½ to 2 inches in diameter. If left too long they
will have a woody taste. To prevent from bleeding, leave on skins
and at least ½ inch of the tops when boiling.

Initial planting, C group

Carrots

Royal Chantenay (recommended variety)
Cylindrical shape with very little taper: Good color, roots red-orange right to the center: Grows to about 5 inches long.
60 days to maturity.
Small seed.

How to plant
Plant in 3 single conventional rows, 4 inches apart:
Make ¼-inch furrows, sow 1 seed every 1 inch.
Curl your forefinger and firm, do not cover, water.

General care
If sown properly, seedlings should be about 1 inch apart. No thinning is necessary at this point. When carrots are pencil size, pull every other one until all those remaining are 2 inches apart. Carrots at this size are large enough to be eaten, so this thinning is really an early harvest. No further thinning is necessary, leave at this spacing for full growth. Keep moist at the roots. Try to maintain an even moisture in the soil. Do not soak. If soil is too wet the carrots will rot. Carrots usually do not need cultivating.

Harvesting
Main harvest when top of carrot root has grown to a diameter of about 1 to 1½ inches. To check just push a little soil away and look at the top of the root. Pull by hand. If left until larger, may not come out. If this happens, use a garden trowel, push down into the soil right next to the root and lever back and forth to loosen. They can then be easily pulled. Carrots are quite hardy and are able to take some frost. Can be left in the ground and harvested, as wanted, up into late fall. In fact, under a shredded leaf mulch they can even overwinter, which will provide a welcome early harvest in the next season.

6

The transition process

As the crops that were sown in the initial planting become fully harvested, it is then time for the succession crops to take their place. This does not happen all at once, as different crops mature at different times. This changeover begins in the spring and extends through the summer.

Procedures

As a general rule, in all cases, when a vegetable has been fully harvested, pull the plants and put into the compost pile. If the plants have thick stems, cut up into small pieces before adding.

After all of the plants have been removed from an area, strip the soil clean. Go over it several times to be sure that all weeds, roots, and any other residues have been removed.

Once you are satisfied that the ground is clear, give a very light cultivation with a rake and smooth out. Then leave it bare.

Transplants

Although most of the succession crops are direct seeded, two of them, tomatoes and broccoli, are put in as transplants.

If you grow your own tomato transplants from seed, they will have been sown indoors at the time of the initial planting. (About six to eight weeks previously.) The plants will be of proper size on their planned transplanting date.

For the broccoli to be at a large seedling size, with three or more true leaves, at its scheduled transplanting date, it will have to be seeded during the transition period (about June 15th). This will in no way affect anything in the garden as the seeds are sown in a small flat that is transportable anywhere.

The transition will occur in the sequence that follows

B group: Make room for the tomatoes, carrots, and bush beans
Tomato transplants are scheduled to go in on the first frost-free day of spring, May 15 in my zone. So the pea vines in the areas where they are to go will have to be pulled. They will have served their purpose as a cover crop. The pods, unfortunately, won't be mature at that time and will be lost on those vines.

But the rest of the pea crop, that in-between the tomato plant units, will remain standing to be harvested at maturity.

There is an option. If you don't want to sacrifice any pods you can delay the setting in of the tomatoes until after all of the peas have been harvested. But this would be about a month later. Some gardeners claim that later is better. I have never done this so don't know if that is true or not. The choice is yours to make.

Once all of the pea vines have been pulled, the space for the second sowing of carrots will be available. This is scheduled for around the middle of June. (But can go in later if need be.)

The sowing of two rows of bush beans, also planned for the same date, will go into the areas that the overwintered parsley and Swiss chard occupied. If they are still standing, pull, as at this point, they would have already served their purpose.

A group: Preparing for the fall crops
Fava beans will be ready in mid- to late June. When they are done producing, pull plants, add to the compost pile, give the bed a light raking, and leave bare.

C group: Pulling garlic and root crops, harvesting salad greens
Garlic should be pulled when a little over half of the tops die back and are dry and yellow (around June 30). Push a trowel down next to the bulb and lever up and down to loosen the soil, then pull. Rub off any dirt and lay the whole plants in an airy dry spot for several weeks to cure. Should be stored at room temperature or cooler. Braid or just tie their stems together and hang up.

MAKING THE TRANSITION

CLEARING OUT THE HARVESTED CROPS AND PREPARING THE MODULES FOR THE SUCCESSION PLANTINGS

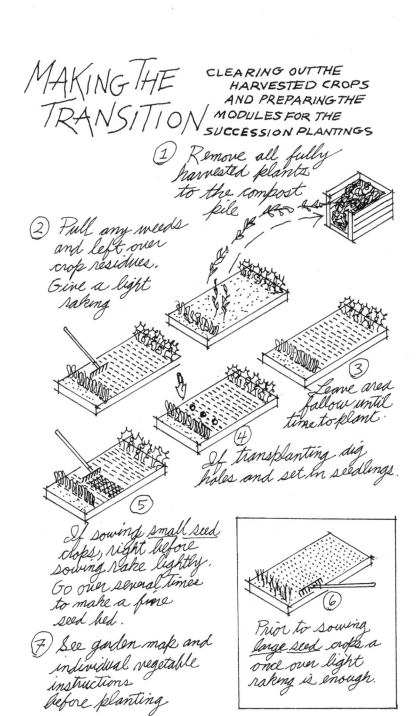

1. Remove all fully harvested plants to the compost pile

2. Pull any weeds and left over crop residues. Give a light raking

3. Leave area fallow until time to plant

4. If transplanting dig holes and set in seedlings.

5. If sowing small seed crops, right before sowing rake lightly. Go over several times to make a fine seed bed.

6. Prior to sowing large seed crops a once over light raking is enough.

7. See garden map and individual vegetable instructions before planting

89

As the days become longer and hotter the spring sowings of arugula, endive, and lettuce will be nearing their peak. But you can slow their decline with extra careful management, and a little luck. It is possible to still be getting salad bowl material up into late July. Water them carefully, late in the afternoon at the roots only. Try not to get any of the leaves wet.

In the event that lettuce plants begin to elongate before the middle of June, a sign that they're going to bolt, cut them off at the base, right inside the lowest leaves slightly above the center core. They should have time to regrow a small head.

If any spring sown carrots and beets are still in the ground on July 30th, all will have to be pulled. The tops of carrots should go into the compost bin. The beet tops are edible and can be eaten raw in salads or cooked as spinach. Then, except for the onions, which stay, final harvest any other C group vegetables that are still standing. When that has been done, begin to prepare the soil for the main sowing of bush beans.

Optional sowing times of bush beans. In the event that some C group crops are fully harvested early, their individual planting units can be sown with bush beans at that time. You don't have to wait until July 30. This will spread out the harvest.

Good garden hygiene

During this transition period it is a good time to look over the entire garden to make sure that good garden hygiene is still being practiced. As we get deeper into the season the tendency is to get a little lax.

Remind yourself of these basics:

1) Keep the garden clean; do not let rotting fruits or any other decaying material lie on the soil.

2) Get rid of diseased or dying plants. They will only spread disease further and attract bugs. Also pinch off any yellowing or dead leaves on plants.

3) Pull weeds, cultivate if needed to keep soil from crusting.

4) Keep an even soil moisture.

5) Stay out of the garden when plants are wet. Bacteria or fungus spores can be present in the moisture that is on the leaves. By touching plants as you walk, you can be spreading diseases. If you must go in when plants are wet just be extra careful.

7

The succession planting

Once the vegetables in the initial planting have completed their production and are fully harvested, their places become available. After the areas have been stripped clean, raked over, and smoothed out, the succession plantings can begin.

Procedures
The succession planting consists of both warm season and cool season vegetables. It will take place over an extended period of time, starting in the spring and continuing into midsummer.

The warm season vegetables, tomatoes and bush beans, will be put in when soil temperatures are in their safe zone. There should not be any difficulty getting them off to a good start.

However, the cool season vegetables that are planted in the summer are often confronted with soil temperatures higher than is favorable for their germination and good growth. Therefore extra steps must be taken if the summer plantings are to be successful. The procedures for the succession planting to be followed are given below.

Broccoli transplants
Broccoli will be set in as transplants on its scheduled planting date. For the seedlings to be of transplanting size on that date they will have to be started in a flat on about June 15. I use a half-gallon milk carton, cut lengthwise and filled with a 50-50 mix of compost and soil. (Be sure to punch holes in the bottom for

drainage.) Since 8 are needed, plant 12 for insurance. Plant seeds ½ inch deep, 1 inch apart within rows, 2 inches apart. Water with a hand spray, put in a shady location until they sprout, then move to a sunny spot. Water the seedlings daily at the roots.

Hot weather sowing of cool season crops
Since the sowing of the succession planting cool season crops will be done in the middle of July, be aware that, for most, the ideal soil temperature for their germination is 65–75° F. Below or above that range will affect the time and rate of germination. When soil heats up to 80°F and above, some of these seeds are adversely affected. Lettuce is one of them, and at a soil temperature of 80°F or above it will not germinate.

The sowing procedure is basically the same as for the initial planting but needs to be modified as follows:

1) Put seed in the freezer 2 days before planting. Take out right before it is time to plant. Sow in the late afternoon when the sun is low and the temperature has dropped a little.

2) Make furrows slightly deeper than the spring depths. This will result in more coverage above the seed, giving it more protection from the sun's hot rays.

3) Before sowing, thoroughly soak the furrow.

4) Sow the seed in the furrow. Curl your forefinger, and with the part between the first and second joints, press it into the soil.

5) After firming the seed in the furrows, cover lightly with loose compost (except endive, which needs light to germinate).

6) Wet down again with a spray.

7) Then, shade with cardboard "tents" (pieces of cardboard folded into an "A" shape, as shown in the illustration on the facing page). Keep shaded to hold the moisture in the ground and to moderate soil temperatures until germination.

Once seeds germinate and the seedlings are up, remove the tents. The plants will now need some sun. <u>Some</u> is the key word here. The full hot summer rays will cause rapidly rising soil temperatures and adversely affect the young seedlings. Use lath panels to partially shade the plants during the hot weather. (See pages 93, 158, 160–163.)

The soil dries out very quickly in hot dry weather. An even soil moisture must be maintained. Water little but often.

HOTWEATHER DIRECT SEEDING

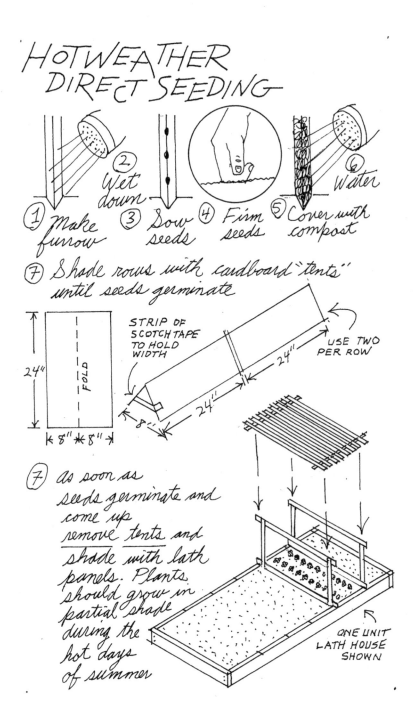

② Wet down

① Make furrow   ③ Sow seeds   ④ Firm seeds   ⑤ Cover with compost   ⑥ Water

⑦ Shade rows with cardboard "tents" until seeds germinate

24"

FOLD

← 8" → ← 8" →

STRIP OF SCOTCH TAPE TO HOLD WIDTH

USE TWO PER ROW

24"

24"

8"

⑦ as soon as seeds germinate and come up remove tents and shade with lath panels. Plants should grow in partial shade during the hot days of summer

ONE UNIT LATH HOUSE SHOWN

Succession planting schedule

As mentioned before, the succession planting is not only of warm season crops but also of cool season crops that will mature in the fall. This planting is done in four stages. First, tomato transplants are set in. Then they are followed in three phases by late summer and fall crops.

First transplanting (about May 15):
    B group Tomatoes—setting in the transplants
First sowing (about June 15th):
    A group Broccoli Transplants—sowing seeds in a flat
    B group Carrots
    B group Bush Beans
Second sowing and transplanting (about July 15):
    A group Endive
    A group Leaf Lettuce
    A group Arugula
    A group Bibb Lettuce
    A group Broccoli—setting in the transplants
    A group Radishes (intercropped with broccoli)
Third sowing (about July 30):
    C group Bush Beans

Set out transplants and sow in the late afternoon when the sun is not too hot. Water transplants at the roots only.

Freshly sown areas are usually watered with the impulse sprinkler. However, when a seeded area abuts an established crop this is not possible. In these cases water the maturing vegetables with the watering wand, adjusted to a flow, holding it at ground level. Then for the newly seeded area, adjusted to a spray, hold the head about 12 to 18 inches above the ground so that the water arcs up and falls like rainfall.

The tomato is a special vegetable and in the modular garden is grown in a special way. This being so, it necessitates a very detailed discussion, which begins on the next page.

Post-succession planting schedule (About October 15):
C group—Garlic. Planted in current B group bed, which will become the C group bed the following season.

Succession planting, B group

Tomatoes

An early variety and a main crop variety are planted.

Earliana (recommended variety)
Starts producing early: Fruits are bright red, 5 to 6 ounces, and set
in clusters. Indeterminate vines.
62 days to maturity.
Small seed.

Delicious (recommended variety)
Produces large, smooth, red meaty fruits that are crack-resistant:
Can grow to one pound or more. Indeterminate vines.
77 days to maturity.
Small seed.

How to plant
Although tomatoes can be direct seeded in the garden the results
are very unpredictable. They are best set out as transplants. Transplants can be grown from seed indoors about 6 to 8 weeks before
the outdoor planting date, or they can be purchased anytime prior
to outdoor planting at your local gardening center.

Growing your own transplants from seed is by far the most
cost-effective and best method. Not only does it save money, but
it will result in stronger, healthier, disease-free plants.

Starting from seed
To grow your own transplants, prepare a planting medium in
the previous fall. In a 2½- to 3-gallon pail, mix together equal
amounts of good garden soil and finished compost. Cover with
a plastic bag to retain the moisture and set aside indoors to age.
Several days before the scheduled sowing date, bring the medium
into a well heated room to warm it up. Never sow in a cold mix.

A flat can be as simple as a half-gallon milk carton cut
lengthwise or any other shallow container. Punch holes in the

bottom to allow for drainage. Use two flats, one for each variety.

Fill the flats with the planting medium and level. Next, sift some well aged compost through a ⅛-inch screen and spread a thin layer over the surface. Before sowing examine seeds. Pick out the roundest plumpest ones. These represent a better parcel of nutrients and will give the seedlings a head start.

Sow at least 50 percent more than you need. Just place them on the surface in two rows that are 2 inches apart: Space seed every ½ inch within rows. Press them into the soil with your fingertip, cover very lightly. Spray with a hand spray so that the mix is moist, <u>not waterlogged</u>. Always use tepid, not cold, water.

Place the flats into a clear plastic bag and keep it in bright light, but not in the sun. As soon as they germinate and start to show (they will be white, not green) remove from the plastic bag and put them in a south window where they will receive direct sunlight all day. As they grow snip off spindly plants at ground level so that those remaining are about 1 inch apart.

Keep soil moist, not soaked. Too wet and you risk them collapsing and dying from a condition called "damping off."

The first two leaves on the plant are "seed leaves." They are elongated, oval-shaped, and not true leaves. When the seedlings have two or three well-developed true leaves, select strongest, best plants and transplant into individual containers. I use tin cans.

Fill with the same 50-50 mix of soil and compost as was used in the flats. Again, punch holes in the bottoms. Go to the flat and using a plastic knife cut out a square that contains the roots around each seedling. Lift the square out with the tip of the knife, retaining as much soil as possible, plant deep right up to the seed leaves. To prevent them from wilting, keep out of the sun for a day. Then return to the south window.

To build up the plants, every day brush them lightly with your hand. Just gently bend them over to a slight angle then let them spring back. This slight stress will cause them to develop thicker and stockier stems.

Hardening off
Before transplants can be set out, they must be hardened off, a process to toughen them for the harsher environment of the outdoors. About a week before the transplanting date, on a calm

TOMATO TRANSPLANTS

GROWING FROM SEED

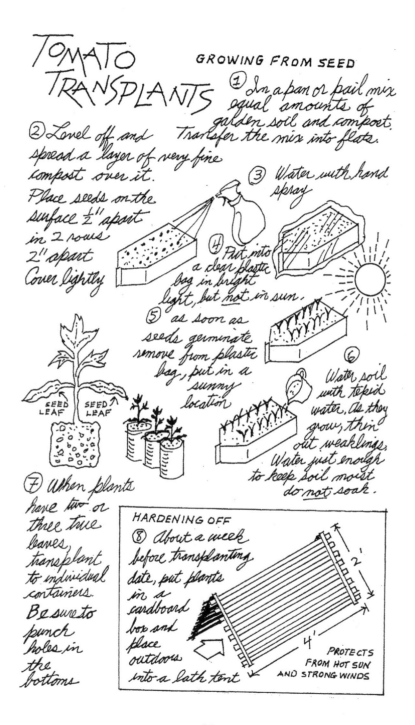

① In a pan or pail mix equal amounts of garden soil and compost. Transfer the mix into flats.

② Level off and spread a layer of very fine compost over it. Place seeds on the surface ½" apart in 2 rows 2" apart Cover lightly

③ Water with hand spray

④ Put into a clear plastic bag in bright light, but not in sun.

⑤ as soon as seeds germinate remove from plastic bag, put in a sunny location

SEED LEAF   SEED LEAF

⑥ Water soil with tepid water. As they grow, thin out weaklings. Water just enough to keep soil moist do not soak.

⑦ When plants have two or three true leaves, transplant to individual containers. Be sure to punch holes in the bottoms

HARDENING OFF

⑧ About a week before transplanting date, put plants in a cardboard box and place outdoors into a lath tent

2'
4'

PROTECTS FROM HOT SUN AND STRONG WINDS

day, when air temperature is at least 60°F, find a warm outdoor spot, erect a lath tent (see page 97), put seedlings in a cardboard box that is about 6 inches high, and place in the tent. Leave them out for an hour or so, then bring them in. The next day leave them out for about two hours. Subsequently, put them out every morning, gradually increasing outdoor time until they can stay out all day before taking them in. On days that are cold and windy do not put them out; it will only set them back. If the weather has remained steady, by the end of the week they should be ready to be set in. A few days before the transplant date, unless there is danger of frost, let them stay out all night, too.

Buying transplants
If buying, look for bushy compact plants with thick stems. The stems should have a purple color. Avoid those that show signs of yellowing, have blemishes, or otherwise have poor color.

Training systems
Before going into the details of setting out the transplants, in order to understand the reasoning behind my system of growing tomatoes, a little general background is necessary.

When I first planted tomatoes, they were staked and tied as they grew. It is a simple, proven method and, to this day, indeed hard to beat. The thing that bothered me was the continuous tying up of the plants. That fact motivated me to try to find a less labor-intensive method. In that search just about everything imaginable was tried: teepees, trellises, poles with arms, poles with ropes, "A" frames, "X" frames, cages, and many other systems. All had some merit but only the cages impressed me as being any better than the simple stake. They eliminated the work of tying, but each plant, having its own cage, took up a lot of space.

It seemed to me that this did not have to be. If a cage could be built in such a way to contain and give support to more than one plant, less space would be required.

I had been planting 12 tomato plants, 18 inches apart in rows 24 inches apart. This arrangement filled a full module—why not enclose all in one big cage? I made six 4-foot poles and drove nails in them sticking out at a slight angle, one low, one in the center, and one near the top.

These posts were then driven into the ground at each corner of the module and one at each side in the middle. Then 8-foot 1x2s were placed on the protruding lowest nails joining the three posts on each side. Next, 4-foot laths were placed across, resting on these strips, forming a latticework for the plants to grow up into. As the plants grew the vines were supported on the laths.

When they grew taller another tier of supports was added, using the center nails on the posts. Then a final tier using the top nails. Simply put, the plants were enclosed in the framework of a big rectangular box, with interior supports. The plants grew naturally and required no tying.

The system worked fairly well and I kept using it for about four or five years.

But one big cage was not really practical. Some rethinking, evaluations, adjustments, and further trials were called for.

Cluster planting

Since two varieties of tomatoes were regularly being planted, Earliana and Delicious, I reasoned that instead of one big cage, why not separate the two varieties and build two smaller cages? This approach would also utilize the area more efficiently.

To do this the plants would have to be spaced much closer, in clusters. So six were planted near one end of the module and another six near the other end. I then observed them as they grew to determine what kind of cages would be needed.

It soon became apparent that the most efficient shape would be a rectangle. In other words, my one big cage scaled down to a smaller size. As they grew the cages were built around them much the same as had been done with the larger version.

Although the plants were closer together in the clusters than they were when they occupied the full module, it didn't seem to have any detrimental effect; in fact, they appeared to benefit from this closeness. The soil retained moisture better due to the increased shade, no blossom end rot was apparent, and neither was any sun scald on the fruits.

I was convinced that this was the way to go. Modifications and improvements were continually made each year until an acceptable result was had. The final cage is described and illustrated on the following pages.

Cluster cage

The cluster cage is a rectangular framework designed to support a cluster of tomato plants. Assembled it is 2 feet wide by 4 feet tall by 4 feet long. It has three tiers of supports. Materials used in its construction are 1x2 furring strips, $1\frac{1}{4}$-inch x #6 deck screws, and $\frac{1}{4}$- x $2\frac{1}{2}$-inch bolts with washers and wing nuts.

A cage requires two 2- x 4-foot post units. Each post unit consists of two 4-foot posts joined together by three 2-foot support bars spaced 12 inches apart. When assembled, the two post units are connected by 4-foot stringers, two of which have legs they are called stabilizer units. Three stringers make up a tier. Two 2-foot-divider bars are placed at measured points on the stringers of each tier to form six open spaces.

To construct a post unit: Two are needed for each cage. Take two 4-foot lengths of furring strips to be the posts. Measuring from one end, which will be the bottom, make marks at 9 inches, 21 inches, and 33 inches, then measure down 2 inches from the top and drill a $\frac{1}{4}$-inch hole. Place the two posts on the floor 2 feet apart, outside edge to outside edge.

Then place 2-foot lengths on the posts, lining up top edges with the marks, and fasten to the posts using $1\frac{1}{4}$-inch #6 deck screws. On their tops, in the center and at the point where they meet the posts, cut $\frac{3}{4}$ inch-wide by $\frac{1}{2}$ inch-deep notches.

To make a stringer: Nine are needed for each cage. Take a 4-foot length of furring strip, measure $16\frac{1}{2}$ inches from each end and cut square notches $\frac{3}{4}$ inch wide by $\frac{1}{2}$ inch deep. This is the top of the stringer. On the opposite side, the bottom, measure over 1 inch from each end and cut the same size square notches.

To make a stabilizer unit: Two are needed for each cage. Take one of the stringers and in the exact center, drill a $\frac{1}{4}$-inch hole. Cut two 30-inch-lengths of furring strip, then drill a $\frac{1}{4}$-inch hole $\frac{3}{4}$ inch from one end of each.

These will be fold down legs. Fasten them both to one side of the stringer by inserting a $\frac{1}{4}$- x $2\frac{1}{2}$-inch bolt through the holes and secure with a washer and wing nut.

To make a divider bar: Six needed for each cage. Take a 2-foot length of furring strip, measure over $1\frac{1}{2}$ inches from each end, cut square notches $\frac{3}{4}$ inch wide by $\frac{1}{2}$ inch deep. In the exact center, cut another same size notch. This is the bottom of the bar.

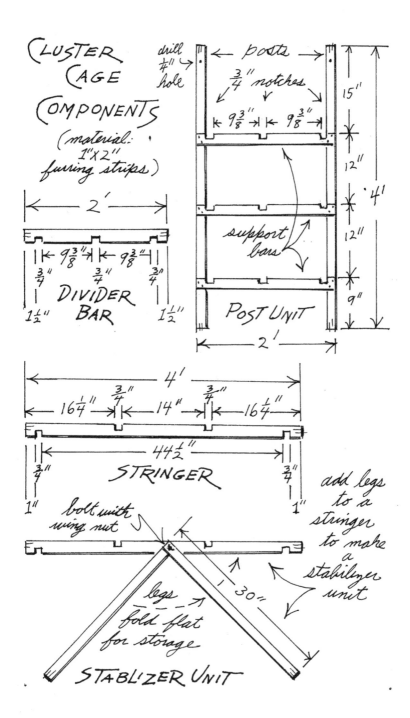

CLUSTER CAGE COMPONENTS

(material: 1"X2" furring strips)

drill ¼" hole

← posts →

¾" notches

9⅜" ← 9⅜"

15"

12"

4'

support bars

12"

9"

POST UNIT

2'

2'

DIVIDER BAR

9⅜" ← 9⅜"

¾" ¾" ¾"

1½" 1½"

4'

16¼" ¾" 14" ¾" 16¼"

44½"

STRINGER

¾" ¾"

1" 1"

add legs to a stringer to make a stabilizer unit

bolt with wing nut

legs fold flat for storage

30"

STABLIZER UNIT

The illustration on page 101 shows all construction details. To prevent rotting, it is recommended that all of the cluster cage components be treated with a nontoxic water sealer.

Assembling a cluster cage in a module
The cluster cages are not put up until the tomato plants are approximately two feet tall. By that time a mulch should already be in place. If not, put one down before proceeding any further. The cages are erected as follows:

1) Take a stabilizer unit. Loosen wing nut, lower and spread the legs across width of the module so that the tips of each touch the inside of the module frame. Tighten the wing nut snug.

2) Position a post unit at one side of the module, support bars facing out to the side. Unit should be 12 inches from end.

3) Holding the post unit upright, notch one of the stabilizing unit's end notches into the support bar notch by the post. Press the legs into the ground to keep the post unit from falling.

4) Go to the other side. Position the other post unit directly across. Take the loose end of the stabilizer unit and notch the end notch into the support bar notch as was done on the first side.

5) Using the same procedure, erect the other stabilizer unit so that both post units are connected. Then adjust the legs so that the structure is erect and stable.

6) Add the first tier by notching three stringers into the proper notches on the lower support bars: One on each side and one in the center. Then add the divider bars by matching up their notches with the ones on the stringer bars.

7) Add second and third tiers as needed. The second tier, already having the stringers of the stabilizer units, needs only the center stringer and the divider bars added. The third tier requires all three stringers and the divider bars.

8) If plants grow to the top, give support by threading a piece of clothesline through the holes to form a rectangular loop. Then tie the ends together.

Take care, especially with the first tier, not to injure the plants. When putting in the stringers, slide them in from the ends, lifting any branches that may be in the way.

Slide the divider bars in from the sides again taking care to lift any branches as may be necessary. When the tier is fully

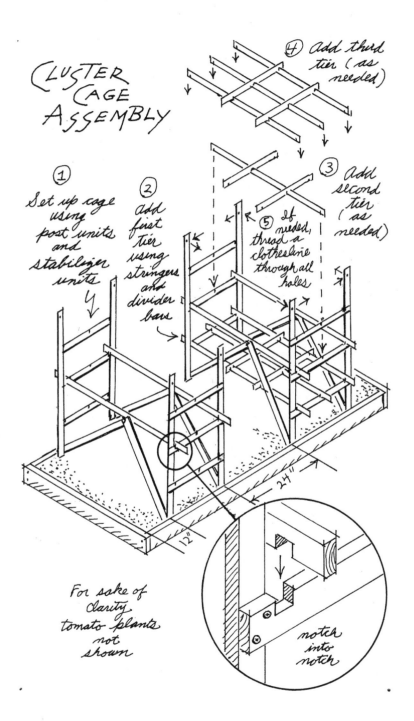

CLUSTER CAGE ASSEMBLY

④ Add third tier (as needed)

① Set up cage using post units and stabilizer units ↓

② Add first tier using stringers and divider bars →

③ Add second tier (as needed)

⑤ If needed, thread a clothesline through all holes

24"

12"

For sake of clarity, tomato plants not shown

notch into notch

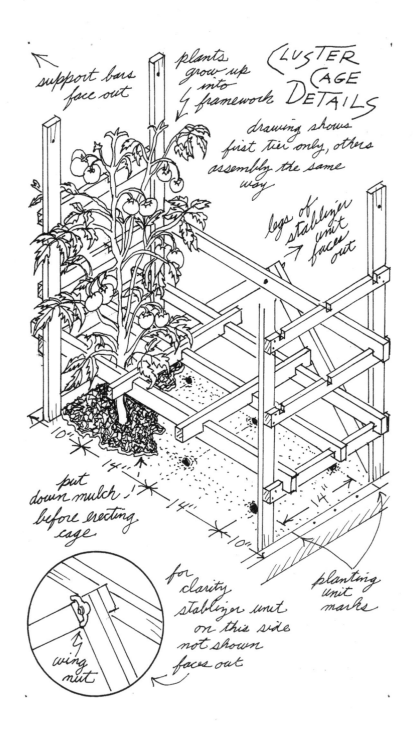

support bars face out

plants grow up into framework

CLUSTER CAGE DETAILS

drawing shows first tier only, others assembly the same way

legs of stablizer unit faces out

put down mulch! before erecting cage

10"

14"

14"

14"

10"

for clarity stablizer unit on this side not shown faces out

wing nut

planting unit marks

installed, the branches should be resting on those supports. The illustrations on pages 101,103, and 104 show construction, plus assembly details. *(Besides cluster cages there are three other tomato training methods that I can recommend, see page 178.)*

Note: Furring strips have been specified because they are cheap. Regular 1x2 lumber will cost more but will give you a better job and is recommended.

Once the training method is known, the tomato transplants can be set into their designated planting units.

But first, since tomatoes follow peas as a succession planting, the pea vines standing in those units will have to be removed to make room for them. They will have served their purpose as a cover crop, having added nitrogen to the soil.

Sadly, the pods on those vines will not be of harvestable size and will be lost. I know, it will tug at your heart, but just grit your teeth, pull them out, and add them to the compost pile.

A pea harvest will still be had as the rest of the crop, that in-between those planting units, will remain and be harvested.

Setting out the transplants

Once the pea vines, and any weeds that may have grown, have been pulled, rake the area smooth.

In the morning of the transplanting day, water the plants thoroughly in their containers. This will help keep the root ball from breaking apart. If some plants have developed blossoms, remove them before setting in. This may seem contrary to logic but if left on, the root system will not develop properly.

Bright sun can harm newly set-in transplants. Ideally you should transplant on a cloudy day. This, of course, is not always feasible. The next best time is in the late afternoon, when the sun has started to decline and has lost some of its heat. Try to keep the roots in your shadow when they are out of their containers.

Plant in two clusters of six: each cluster in its designated planting unit, two single rows to a cluster, rows 14 inches apart, plants spaced 14 inches apart in the rows.

Measure and mark the positions where the plants are to go. Dig holes, about twice the width and twice the depth of the containers that hold the transplants. Don't skimp. Throw a couple of handfuls of compost into the bottom of the holes.

Remove transplants from their containers by turning them upside down, holding them so that the stem is in-between your forefinger and middle finger, then give a sharp tap on the bottom. Usually they will come out easily. If they don't, run a knife around between the soil and the container and try again.

After removing from container, inspect the root ball. If roots are matted or circling around the root ball, with a knife or razor blade make vertical cuts up the sides and horizontal cuts across the bottom of the ball. This will cause the roots to grow outward into the surrounding soil. Otherwise, sometimes they will just stay in that little ball greatly retarding the growth of the plant. To avoid soil borne diseases, do not let any leaves touch the ground.

Before planting remove first pair of the lowest leaves. Set in transplants so that the remaining second pair of lower leaves are just above but not touching the soil. If plants are leggy, remove two or three pairs of leaves, plant up to remaining bottom leaves.

Remove any air pockets by firming soil around root ball with your fingers. Leave a slight depression at the surface. Pour about a quart of water around the base of the plant, then fill with dry soil. For cutworm protection, use a 3-inch-wide strip of stiff paper to form a circle around the stem. Sink this "collar"1 inch into the soil and leave 2 inches above. Hold together with a paper clip.

General care

Do not let the soil crust up, cultivate around plants to keep the soil loose and porous. Late in the afternoon, about two hours before sunset, water with the watering wand at the roots only.

Blights are a big problem when growing tomatoes. They are spread by soil being splashed onto the leaves. You can go a far way in controlling these diseases if, as soon as the soil has been warmed up, you cover the entire area under the plants with a mulch. This will minimize the spread of blight by preventing soil splash. Just remember not to apply the mulch too soon.

Tomatoes need a thoroughly warmed up soil to grow well. The mulch can be put down once the plants are well established and growing vigorously. Prepare the area by pulling any weeds, then give a shallow cultivation followed by a watering of the ground with the watering wand adjusted to a very slow, soft flowing steady stream. Do not cause any splashing.

TOMATO TRANSPLANTS

SETTING THEM INTO THE GARDEN

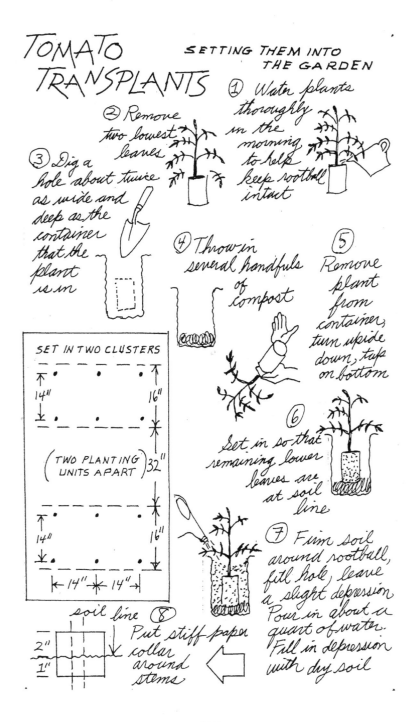

① Water plants thoroughly in the morning, to help keep rootball intact

② Remove two lowest leaves

③ Dig a hole about twice as wide and deep as the container that the plant is in

④ Throw in several handfuls of compost

⑤ Remove plant from container, turn upside down, tap on bottom

⑥ Set in so that remaining lower leaves are at soil line

⑦ Firm soil around rootball, fill hole, leave a slight depression. Pour in about a quart of water. Fill in depression with dry soil

⑧ Put stiff paper collar around stems

SET IN TWO CLUSTERS

14"   16"

(TWO PLANTING UNITS APART) 32"

14"   16"

← 14" → ← 14" →

soil line

2"
1"

Finally spread a 2- to 3-inch layer of shredded leaves, or grass clippings, completely covering the soil under the plants. Mulch must be porous enough so that rain can trickle through.

When plants have grown to about 2 feet tall and are starting to bend over, it is time to put up the cluster cages. If mulch was not previously put down, do it now.

Put up the cluster cages, taking care that the plants are in the proper positions. At this time, only the first tier of supports is necessary. Watch the plants as they continue their growth.

Flowers are pollinated by wind or insects. But a daily gentle shaking of the plants will spread additional pollen, increasing flower set, resulting in more fruit.

When needed add second and third tiers of supports. If plants grow to the top, string a clothesline through the holes to contain.

With the mulch they will not need as much watering. Check under the mulch regularly by poking a forefinger into the soil, it should be moist, but not soggy, for the full length of your finger. If dry, water. If soggy, you're watering too much, cut back.

Harvesting
Harvest all ripe tomatoes as soon as they ripen. Plants should be examined on a regular basis to make sure that all fully ripened tomatoes are removed. Do not allow them to remain on the vine to become too soft. At the end of the season the harvest can be prolonged by pulling up entire plants and hanging them by the roots in a sheltered place. The fruits will continue to ripen even after the vines have wilted.

A less dramatic way of prolonging the harvest is to pick all of the green tomatoes that are starting to change color, even if only to a lighter shade of green. Pick bright green ones only if you intend to pickle or fry them, otherwise don't bother. Any tomatoes stored should be free of cuts or cracks in the skin that will allow decay to set in and ruin the fruit. In a fairly dark place spread them out in a cardboard box. Cover with paper and check regularly to see which ones are getting ripe. The ripening process can be speeded up by placing a few in a brown paper bag.

After harvesting, if plants show any signs of infection, do not put them in the compost bin; that will spread the infection to other crops. Burn or dispose of them by other means.

Succession planting, B group

Carrots

Royal Chantenay (recommended variety)
Cylindrical shape with very little taper: Good color, roots red-orange right to the center. Grow to about 5 inches long.
60 days to maturity. Small seed.

How to plant
Plant in 3 single conventional rows, 4 inches apart.
Make ¼-inch furrows, sow 1 seed every 1 inch.
Curl your forefinger and firm. Do not cover, water.

General care and harvesting: Same as for the initial planting on page 86, except that, if desired, you can: 1) Prolong the harvest by leaving the carrots in the ground and pulling only as needed, 2) Leave some, or all, of them to overwinter. (Must be mulched.)

Succession planting, B group

Bush Beans

Bush Blue Lake (recommended variety)
Dark green, round pods average 6 inches long: Unique flavor, slow fiber and seed development. Dwarf bushy plants.
55 days to maturity. Large seed.

How to plant
Plant in 2 single rows: one row, at each end of the module. Make ¼-inch furrows, sow seeds 3 inches apart. With a forefinger push seeds about 1 inch deeper into the soil. Cover with compost or soil, firm, and water. <u>Do not overwater.</u>

General care: Once established, water at roots and keep the soil from crusting. Harvesting: Same as for main sowing: (See page 115.)

Succession planting, A group

Endive

Green Curled (recommended variety)
Dark, finely cut leaves: Slightly bitter taste. Excellent for use in mixed greens salads.
90 days to maturity. Small seed.

How to plant
Plant in 1 triplex row, side by side with leaf lettuce.
Make ¼-inch furrows, wet them down, sow 1seed every 1 inch. Do not cover seed, it is light sensitive. Firm, water with spray, and then shade.

General care and harvesting
Basically the same as for the initial planting (see page 82).

Succession planting, A group

Leaf Lettuce

Simpson Elite (recommended variety)
Light lime green, crinkled leaves: Similar to the old favorite Black-Seeded Simpson. Grows well in the fall.
41 days to maturity. Small seed.

How to plant
Plant in 1 triplex row, side by side, with endive.
Make ¼-inch furrows, wet them down, sow 1 seed every 1 inch.
Firm, cover lightly with loose compost, water with spray, and shade.

General care and harvesting
Basically the same as for the initial planting (see page 81).

Succession planting, A group

Bibb Lettuce

Buttercrunch (recommended variety)
Medium green forms a loose head. Thick crisp leaves: long standing, very reliable.
60 days to maturity. Small seed.

How to plant
Plant in 1 triplex row, side by side with arugula.
Make ¼-inch furrows, wet them down, sow 1 seed every 1 inch.
Firm, cover lightly with loose compost, water with spray. Shade to protect from drying out.

General care and harvesting
Basically the same as for the initial planting (see page 84).

Succession planting, A group

Arugula

Astro II (recommended variety)
Dark green, wide, tongue-shaped leaves: A good green for mesclun. Has a strong spicy taste, gives a peppery flavor. 40 days to maturity. Small seed.

How to plant
Plant in 1 triplex row, side by side with bibb lettuce.
Make ¼-inch furrows, wet them down, sow 1 seed every 1 inch.
Firm, cover lightly with loose compost, water with spray, shade.

General care and harvesting
Basically the same as for the initial planting (see page 83).

Succession planting, A group intercrop

Radishes

Comet (recommended variety—but try others)
Round in shape. Advertised to develop normally when planted in midsummer. But I have found that this is not always true. 25 days to maturity. Small seed.

How to plant
Plant in 2 single rows, 1 row on each side of where center row of broccoli will go. Each row spaced 6 inches from that center point. Make ¾-inch furrows. Wet down, sow 1 seed every 2 inches. Curl your forefinger and firm. Cover with compost, water, shade.

General care and harvesting, same as described for Champion radishes (see page 75).

Succession planting, A group

Broccoli Transplants

Broccoli is best handled as transplants. In the middle of June sow seeds in a flat filled with a 50-50 mix of compost and garden soil. (For drainage make sure that the flat has holes in the bottom.) Plant in two rows, 2 inches apart. Sow seeds ½-inch deep every 1 inch within rows.

Eight plants are needed, but to make sure that you have enough good ones, plant at least 4 extras.

Water with a hand spray, then place in a shaded location to germinate. As soon as they sprout move them to a sunny spot. (Putting them in a lath tent will provide a cooler more favorable growing atmosphere.)

Keep the soil moist. As they grow, thin out weak plants. By the time they are scheduled to go into the garden they should have developed three or more true leaves.

BROCCOLI TRANSPLANTS

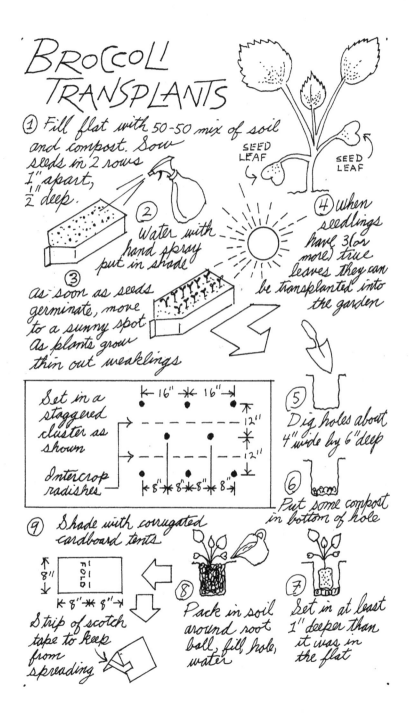

① Fill flat with 50-50 mix of soil and compost. Sow seeds in 2 rows 1" apart, ½" deep.

SEED LEAF

SEED LEAF

② Water with hand spray put in shade

④ When seedlings have 3 (or more) true leaves they can be transplanted into the garden

③ as soon as seeds germinate, move to a sunny spot. As plants grow thin out weaklings

Set in a staggered cluster as shown

Intercrop radishes

←16"→ ←16"→
12"
12"
←8"→8"→8"→8"→

⑤ Dig holes about 4" wide by 6" deep

⑥ Put some compost in bottom of hole

⑨ Shade with corrugated cardboard tents

↑8"↓ FOLD ←8"→8"→

Strip of scotch tape to keep from spreading

⑧ Pack in soil around root ball, fill hole, water

⑦ Set in at least 1" deeper than it was in the flat

113

Succession planting, A group

Broccoli

De Cicco (recommended variety)
Light green plants produce 3- to 4-inch central heads followed by
a long harvest of side shoots: Variable maturity.
48–85 days to maturity.
Small seed.

Setting out the transplants
Make three furrows as guide lines. One at center planting unit saw
mark and 2 others, spaced 12 inches on each side. Measure and
mark positions where transplants are to go. They will be spaced
16 inches apart in staggered rows. Two in the center row, three in
the other two rows. (See illustration on previous page.)
   Transplant in the late afternoon when the sun is low. Several hours prior to that, thoroughly water flats to keep soil intact
when lifting out. Dig holes about 4 inches wide by 6 inches deep.
Throw some compost in the bottom. Set seedling in the hole at
least 1 inch deeper than it was in the flat. Pack soil around the
roots, water at the stem's base. Shade for the first full day in the
sun to lessen the stress of transplanting.

General care
Once well established put down a 2- to 3-inch shredded leaf
mulch over the entire area under the plants.

Harvesting
Harvest before flower buds begin to open. If allowed to open, the
plant will stop producing. Cut just below the bud cluster while the
buds are still light, before they start producing tiny yellow flowers. After the main head is cut, small side shoots will grow from
where the leaves meet the stems. The plant will keep producing
these side shoots until freezing weather, as long as the shoots are
never cut back to the main stem. Leave the base of the shoot and
a couple of leaves on each stem. New shoots will grow from these
leaf junctions. Light frosts improve the flavor.

Succession planting, C group

Bush Beans

Bush Blue Lake (recommended variety)
Dark green, round pods average 6 inches long: Unique flavor,
slow fiber and seed development. Dwarf bushy plants.
55 days to maturity. Large seed.

How to plant
Plant in staggered rows, 4 inches apart.
Make ¼-inch furrows, sow seeds 4 inches apart. Using a
forefinger, push seeds farther into the soil, about 1 inch.
Cover the entire furrow with compost, water. <u>Do not overwater.</u>

Optional early sowings
If individual planting units become vacant before July 30, they
can be sown with bush beans as soon as they are available. Units
still occupied will be sown after their final harvest, which in most
cases is usually right before July 30.

General care
No thinning is necessary. Sprouts should stand, as seeds were
sown, 4 inches apart. Due to the close spacing, as the plants develop they will shade the ground, suppressing weed growth. Pull
out any weeds that come up. Once seedlings are established, water
at the roots late in the afternoon. Do not let dry out. Inspect daily
for Mexican bean beetles. Hand pick adults, and destroy eggs and
any larvae that you see.

Harvesting
Harvest while pods are immature and before they have finished
growing. Seeds should be small and the bean should snap when
you break it. Beans have to be watched; should be picked when
they are large enough to eat but before the flesh gets tough and
the beans make lumps in the pods. If pods are allowed to ripen
fully, the plants will stop producing and die. If care is taken, many
pickings can be had from a planting.

Autumn Leaves

With the sowing of bush beans the succession plantings have been completed. But there is still a post-succession planting to do —garlic. It will not be put in until the earliest frost date or later. Garlic is not, per se, a succession planting as it will be harvested in the next season.

As we approach the autumn season it is time to start thinking about collecting the falling leaves that will be used for mulching the beds and also as "browns" in the compost pile.

Leaves used for mulching should be shredded so that rainwater or melting snow can trickle through to the ground. This can be done by piling them near a fence or wall (to contain them) and running them over with a power mower.

Large plastic bags are really the only practical way to store leaves until ready for use. Those to be used for composting should also be shredded, otherwise they will mat down. For convenience, stockpile those bags near the compost bin. Their decomposition process can be speeded up by throwing in a little soil and spraying lightly with water.

Once the little odds and ends have been taken care of, the focus can turn to finalizing the fall wrap-up. This is a gradual process. As subsequent crops are harvested and their residues put into the compost bin, appropriate action is taken to ready the beds for the oncoming cold weather.

The role of garlic in the fall wrap-up

Although garlic can be planted in the spring, it is best planted in the fall for harvest the following year. Cloves need to be exposed to low temperatures to have their dormancy broken, otherwise they may not produce bulbs. Spring planting produces small bulbs.

This setting in of the garlic cloves is, in effect, both the last planting of the present season and the first of the next, as they will sprout before any of the new initial planted crops.

Since the proper time for the setting in of the cloves is the earliest fall frost date or later, this factor will determine when the final winterizing of its bed can be accomplished.

Post-succession planting, C group *(fall planted in B group bed— which will become the C group bed the next season).*

Garlic

Variety: Elephant (or use that sold in supermarkets)
Very large, mild cloves: They are very white on the outside, light brown skin on the cloves.
90 to 120 days to maturity from date of sprouting in the spring.
No seed available, plant cloves.

How to plant (earliest fall frost date or later)
Plant in 3 staggered single rows, 4 inches apart.

Make ¼-inch deep furrows as guidelines and plant at 6-inch intervals in staggered rows. Break bulbs into cloves. Do not use any small thin ones. If soil is soft enough just push them in, points up and 2 inches below the surface. Fill indentions, water.

If earth is hard, with a trowel, dig 3–4-inch-deep holes. Place cloves in the holes points up and 2 inches below the surface. Firmly pack soil around clove, water, finish filling hole.

General care (for fall and following season)
Once they have been put in, cover the area with a shredded leaf mulch. By the spring the garlic tops will have come up, some poking through the mulch. Remove most of the shredded leaves slowly over a period of several weeks. Leave a thin layer to hold in soil moisture. Pinch off any seed heads that may develop in the spring or summer to increase bulb size, Water when the onions are being watered. Needs very little care and is free from pests and diseases. In fact, it repels pests.

Harvest (early summer)
When a little over half of the tops die back and are dry and yellow, harvest. Push a trowel down into the soil next to the bulb and lever up and down, loosening the earth. Then lift out, rub off any dirt that clings. Lay the whole plants in an airy, dry spot for several weeks to cure. Store at room temperature or cooler (55–60°F). Braid or just tie their stems together and hang up.

8

Preparing for winter

With the arrival of fall, be very mindful of the first frost date. It is the indicator that the growing season is coming to an end.

Tender plants will be killed by just a light frost, 32° to 29°F. Most semi-hardy and hardy plants will survive, but a moderate frost, 28° to 25°F, will affect them too. None of them can live through a hard frost, 24°F or lower, unless protected.

Predicting frost can be done to a certain extent. If the temperature in the late afternoon is above 41°F there probably will be no frost. On the other hand if it is below 36°F there is a very good chance that the ground will be glossy with white the next morning.

With this firmly in mind, the crops must be harvested in a timely manner and the emptied modules prepared for the coming cold months. This is an important step for the garden's well being. Care taken now will pay off in better planting and growing conditions next season.

At this stage, garden hygiene becomes extra important. The fall clean up can be an effective pest control step. If done thoroughly it is possible to greatly reduce the number that will overwinter. As soon as the harvesting of a crop is finished and before most insects have left their host plants, pull them. Strip the area clean. Make sure that the soil is completely bare, no weeds, no crop residues, no roots, absolutely nothing. Then go over the soil with a rake giving a one- to two-inch shallow cultivation.

Leave the plot bare for a few weeks. This will give the birds

WINDING DOWN

HARVESTING, CLEANING UP, PREPARING FOR WINTER

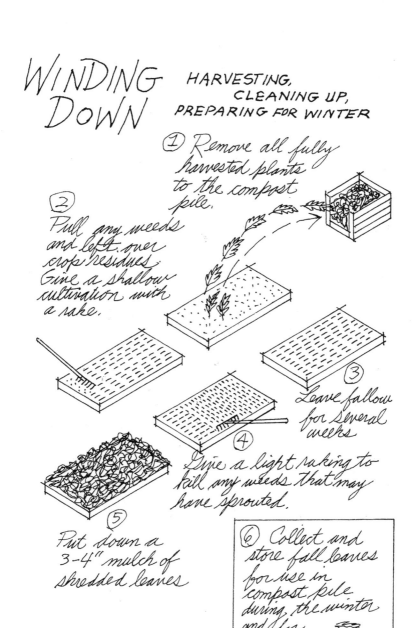

① Remove all fully harvested plants to the compost pile.

② Pull any weeds and left over crop residues. Give a shallow cultivation with a rake.

③ Leave fallow for several weeks

④ Give a light raking to kill any weeds that may have sprouted.

⑤ Put down a 3-4" mulch of shredded leaves

⑥ Collect and store fall leaves for use in compost pile during the winter and for next season.

time to eat any left behind bugs. After the plot has been fallow for two weeks, give another raking, but lighter, to kill any weeds that may have come up and then put down a 3- to 4-inch mulch of shredded leaves.

Leaves can be shredded by lining up piles next to a wall or solid fence and running them over with a rotary lawn mower. The wall or fence will contain them, making collection easy.

Since the vegetables in each crop group are final harvested over differing periods of time the preparing of the individual modules for winter is a slow, spread out, gradual process.

C group: Bush beans and onions

The module containing the C group crops, bush beans and onions, will be the earliest to be completely emptied. Once the bed is totally vacant, follow the procedure just described.

Strip it clean, give a shallow cultivation with a rake, leave the plot fallow for several weeks, then give another light raking and put down a 3- to 4-inch shredded leaf mulch. After it has been completely covered over with the mulch it is all set for the winter. There is nothing further to be done in that module until the beginning of the next season.

B group: Tomatoes, bush beans, carrots, fall planting of garlic

Initial harvest will be the bush bean rows. As the first frost date nears, tomato-growing weather will be rapidly coming to an end. Many gardeners try to protect the plants and keep them standing through frosts. But there is very little to gain by this extra effort.

The cold weather has an adverse effect on the fruits, causing many to become blemished and any additional production to be had is minimal. Instead, a few days before the earliest fall frost date, pick all clean fruit and take them indoors to ripen. Inside a garage or anywhere that affords protection from a frost will do.

Do not bother with any that are cut or cracked as they will rot. Green tomatoes that are starting to change color, even to a lighter shade of green, will in time ripen if properly stored. With that done, pull up all of the plants.

Then you have the option of pulling all of the remaining carrots or leaving them in the ground to be used as needed. If left, there is the additional alternative of letting some or all of them overwinter.

After that has been decided, use a rake to give a deep cultivation over all vacant areas to kill any tomato hornworm pupae that may be in the soil. Allow to remain bare for the next few weeks to expose any other larvae or bugs, then give another raking, but this time very lightly.

Since garlic should be planted on or after the earliest fall frost date, it is put in right after the final raking has been completed. Usually that is the time that the entire module can be covered with a 3- to 4- inch mulch. But if you have left the carrots in the ground—depending on weather conditions—the time line for putting down the mulch may have to be modified. Basically, it is just a matter of not mulching the module too soon for the well-being of the carrots.

Carrots like cool weather, but the mulch must be applied under the right conditions if they are to survive. If after a nightly frost there are many carrot top leaves lying flat on the ground, that is the correct time to cover with the mulch.

Make sure their green tops have adequate coverage. If in doubt, add more. Under the shredded leaves they will not only survive the winter but will have grown to give you an early treat of fresh carrots when the mulch is removed in the spring.

A group: Lettuce, endive, arugula, broccoli, Swiss chard, parsley
The A group succession planting consists entirely of cool season vegetables. All, along with the standing Swiss chard and parsley, can be harvested for as long as they stand up into late fall.

Although the summer sowing was timed so as to be matured by the first frost date, normally they will survive several weeks more without protection. With the addition of a shredded leaf mulch they will survive longer and some may even overwinter.

Lettuce is semi-hardy and can take a few light frosts. For this fall crop, harvest the lettuce the same as was done with the initial planting. But if the plants start to elongate, a sign that they are about to bolt to seed, cut the entire plant at the main stem. Slice off just inside the mature outer bottom leaves, right above the center core, leaving a stub in the ground.

Cut alternate plants first so that not too much bare earth is

121

exposed all at the same time. Then cut those that remain as they are needed. If there is enough favorable weather before a moderate frost, the stub will regrow a small head. Plants can continue to grow and be harvested until depleted or killed by a heavier frost.

Endive and arugula are hardier than lettuce and their fall productive period can be longer. Harvest them, as was done in the initial planting, using the cut-and-come-again technique.

If the weather is not overly severe before a killing frost, all three will continue to supply salad bowl material. Furthermore, endive and arugula, if heavily mulched, may survive the winter. The following spring, upon removal of the mulch they will be pulled, providing early greens.

Swiss chard and parsley, being biennials, are hardy, but not so hardy that they can survive a hard frost without protection. They must be sheltered with a thick mulch to overwinter so as to continue their growth in the following spring.

The mulching of the Swiss chard and parsley must be done carefully if they are to overwinter successfully. Late in the fall when daily temperatures drop below 50°F it is time to start putting on the mulch. Begin by closely surrounding—not covering— the plants with a snug "sheath" of shredded leaves.

You can continue to harvest, as usual, by plucking off the stems of the outer leaves at their base. Just be sure to leave the heart of the plants intact.

Once the temperatures are frequently dipping into the light frost range, it is time to cover over completely with shredded leaves. To be adequately protected make sure that all of the plant is fully covered with mulch.*

If anything is sticking up it will freeze. Since dry leaves are better insulation that wet ones, it is a good idea to put a sheet of clear plastic over the mulch of these two crops. Secure so that it won't blow away and the preparation of the Swiss chard and parsley for the winter is finished.

*Note: The use of modified plant props is the best method of finalizing the mulching of Swiss chard and parsley (see page 163 for explanation).

Broccoli will also withstand some frost and, in fact, a light frost improves its flavor. Under normal fall weather conditions it will stand, without protection, to maturity. However, in the event that an early <u>hard frost</u> is forecast, don't delay—harvest all heads and any shoots that may have developed.

Broccoli is usually the last crop to be fully harvested, the plants pulled and added to the compost pile (their stems are very thick, cut them into small pieces so that they will break down quicker; otherwise they will slow the composting process).

Putting the garden to sleep
The preceding measures are all part of the sequence that slowly prepares the modules for freezing weather. Hard frosts dictate when I cease gardening activities. In my area this is usually around the end of November, but frequently milder temperatures will continue into December.

With the complete covering over of all of the succession planted A group crops, this pretty much brings to a close all end-of-season harvests. Of course, if you dig down through the mulch, some arugula, endive, or carrots may be had, even during the winter.

Every so often, just check the modules to make sure that all have retained enough mulch. If any has been blown away or otherwise dissipated, restore it to its original depth. Otherwise just leave the garden to take a long winter nap.

A time for relaxation and contemplation
Just as a garden needs a rest, so does the gardener. The coming cold months give the opportunity to relax, to enjoy the winter holidays, and to spend more time with family and friends.

The tending and nurturing of vegetables develops traits in a person that make him or her a better human being. So does socializing and developing individual relationships. As with plants, we need a healthy balance in our lives.

If a garden diary is kept, and I believe that everybody should have one, now is the time to go over it and digest the material. There are always surprises. Very seldom do things go exactly as planned. Take note of things that did not work out, what did, and what changes need to be made.

These inactive months are in no way to be considered a negative. They serve a very important function, the re-energizing of both garden and gardener.

9

Crop rotation

The rotation of crops is based on the fact that different crops draw on different nutrients and each is susceptible to different pests and diseases. By rotating your crops all the nutrients are drawn upon, in turn keeping the soil in balance and all pests and soilborne diseases are left without their host crop. A rotation must consider not only the plant itself but also its family and nutrient requirements.

The plants grown fall into the following family groups: *Amaryllidaceae:* garlic, onion. *Chenopodiaceae:* beet, Swiss chard. *Compositae:* endive, lettuce. *Cruciferae:* arugula, broccoli, radish. *Leguminosae:* fava beans, bush beans, peas. *Solanaceae:* tomato. *Umbelliferae:* carrot, parsley.

They also fall into the following approximate nutrient requirement classifications: Heavy feeders: tomato, broccoli, most leaf vegetables, arugula, endive, lettuce, Swiss chard, and parsley. Light feeders: most root crops, carrots, garlic, onions, beets, and radishes. Soil improvers: all of the legumes, bush beans, fava beans, peas; their roots bear nodules that help fix in the soil the nitrogen present in the atmosphere.

There is no one absolute rule for the rotation of crops that I know of. Some follow heavy feeders with light feeders then legumes. Others vary that sequence, putting legumes after heavy feeders followed by light feeders. Still others rotate according to plant size and rooting depth or by alternating slow-growing crops with rapid growers. It can all get very complicated and awfully confusing. But there are some common threads running through most of these theories, and I based my rotation system on these common elements. Generally, crops that have big differences in their feeding requirements should follow one another. In setting up my rotation I kept changing and moving crops around until a practical sequence was arrived at. My final crop rotation system is based on three guidelines:

1) Do not follow a heavy feeder with another heavy feeder. Crops that draw heavily on nutrients, if planted in succession, will soon deplete the soil, resulting in weak, unhealthy plants susceptible to insect attacks and poor soil conditions favorable to weeds.

2) Do not follow any crop with another in its family. Since both will draw upon the same nutrients, the soil will quickly become unbalanced. Instead, follow with a member of a different family. Each crop family draws different nutrients and each contributes something different to improving the soil. Note: Legumes are unique in that they will grow quite well in the same spot for several years in a row. But their nitrogen-adding properties make them especially valuable in rotation with other families.

3) A legume must be a component of each crop group. As "soil improvers" they are vital in a rotation system. They should be inserted between both heavy and light feeders. Besides adding nitrogen, their roots seem to work the soil. They are a major factor in good soil management.

The three separate modules greatly simplify crop rotation. Since the planting areas are separated, soil is not spread from one plot to another, greatly controlling soilborne diseases and pests. It also permits the organizing of crops into groups that remain constant and fill a complete module. Rotation is achieved by moving the entire crop group into a different module each year.

Besides crop rotation, good soil management dictates that the nutrients in the remnants of plants that have been fully harvested be returned to the soil in the form of compost. A regular program of crop rotation, composting, and mulching will ensure that the nutrients in the soil remain balanced.

The chart on page 127 shows the exact rotation. By following each planting unit around the cycle you will see that, aside from bush beans being followed by fava beans, both members of the same family, the guidelines have been adhered to. This was unavoidable because I wanted a legume in each crop group. Anyway, as was mentioned previously, a legume is an exception to the rule and can follow another legume without any negative effects. I believe it to be a valid compromise.

Theoretically, this rotation should minimize the use of nutrients in the soil, help control the spread of soilborne diseases, and disrupt the life cycles of harmful garden pests.

The garden map on pages 68 and 69 shows each crop group in its correct module for the first year. To complete a full rotation cycle the crop groups have to be moved as a unit to a different module at the start of each season.

The crop group in module 1 moves to module 3 and the other two move up one, as follows:

First year
 A group is planted in module 1
 B group is planted in module 2
 C group is planted in module 3
Second year
 B group is now planted in module 1
 C group is now planted in module 2
 A group is now planted in module 3
Third year
 C group is now planted in module 1
 A group is now planted in module 2
 B group is now planted in module 3
Fourth year
 All crop groups are back in their original modules.
 It takes three years to complete a full cycle.

Note: Besides food crops some gardeners also grow compost crops, such as vetch and rye, specifically to provide organic material for the compost pile.

Those who follow this practice will have to add a fourth module and a compost crop group. Using "D" to denote the compost crop group, the rotation sequence would then be:
1st yr.—ABCD: 2nd yr.—BCDA: 3rd yr.—CDAB: 4th yr.—DABC: 5th yr. same as 1st yr. Four years completes a cycle.

CROP ROTATION (It takes 3 years to complete a cycle)

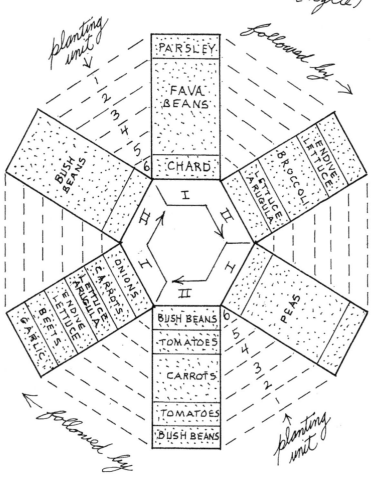

planting unit

followed by

PARSLEY
FAVA BEANS
CHARD

1 2 3 4 5 6

BUSH BEANS

ENDIVE LETTUCE
BROCCOLI
LETTUCE ARUGULA

I
II
I
II
I
II

GARLIC
BEETS
ENDIVE LETTUCE
LETTUCE ARUGULA
CARROTS
ONIONS

BUSH BEANS
TOMATOES
CARROTS
TOMATOES
BUSH BEANS

6 5 4 3 2

PEAS

followed by

planting unit

I Initial Plantings
II Succession Plantings

10

Garden calendar

The calendar on the following pages shows the plantings and harvestings for a complete year. The garden has been planned, through the types of vegetables grown and the timing of the plantings, to give a long continuous harvest from spring into late fall. Harvesting begins with the overwintered crops, then they are joined by early-sown cool-season vegetables. As it gets hot, tomatoes and bush beans enter the procession, producing into fall in conjunction with the late sowings of cool season plants.

In the initial planting all sowings are made as early as safely possible. The hardiest go in about as soon as the soil can be worked: the earlier the sowing, the earlier the harvest. Sowings both in the initial and succession plantings are grouped together as much as possible, reducing labor and conserving water. It requires less effort and water to make a number of sowings all at the same time than to make many individual sowings.

This calendar represents a typical year. The planting and harvesting times may fluctuate from year to year as there are many variables in gardening. The weather, being the biggest variable, does not always do what we would like it to do.

Planting dates are based on my frost zone: average latest frost date is April 20, however, frost is still possible up to May 15. Earliest fall frost is October 15 but usually comes much later.

If your zone generally corresponds to those times, all planting and harvesting dates should pretty much apply. If not, adjust to suit your local conditions.

January

Finish reading seed catalogs.
Finalize selections, order
seeds anytime this month.
Review last season's
garden diary to avoid
repeating any mistakes.

February

Get ready for the new season.
Around the end of the
month, weather permitting,
remove mulch from beds.
Pull and eat any carrots,
arugula, or endive that have
survived the winter.

March

Sow outdoors (about March 15)
Group A: fava beans/radishes.
Group B: peas.
Group C: onions.
Harvest:
Overwintered Swiss chard
and parsley.

April

Sow outdoors (about April 1)
Group A: Swiss chard,
parsley/radishes.
Group C: leaf lettuce,
endive, arugula, bibb lettuce.
Sow indoors (about April 1)
Group B: tomato seeds
(for transplants).
Sow outdoors (about April 15)
Group C: beets, carrots.
Harvest:
Overwintered Swiss chard,
parsley, and radishes.

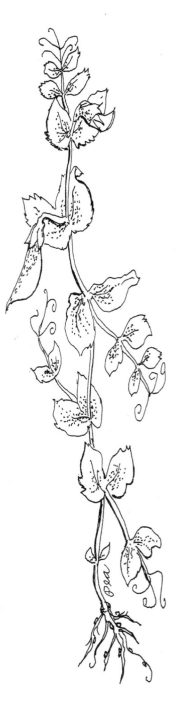

May

Transplant outdoors (about May 15)
> Group B: tomato transplants.

Harvest:
> Swiss chard, parsley, peas,
> radishes, endive, arugula,
> leaf lettuce, bibb lettuce.

June

Sow outdoors (about June 15)
> Group A: broccoli seed
> (in flats).
> Group B: carrots, bush beans.

Harvest:
> Swiss chard, parsley, peas,
> radishes, endive, arugula,
> leaf lettuce, bibb lettuce,
> fava beans, garlic,
> onions/scallions.

July

Sow and transplant* outdoors
(about July 15 or later)
> Group A: endive,
> leaf lettuce, bibb lettuce,
> arugula, radishes, *broccoli.

(about July 30)
> Group C: bush beans.

Harvest:
> Swiss chard, parsley, fava
> beans, tomatoes, beets,
> carrots, endive, leaf lettuce,
> bibb lettuce, onions/scallions.

August

Harvest:
> Swiss chard, parsley,
> tomatoes, bush beans, endive,
> arugula, leaf lettuce, bibb
> lettuce, radish, onions.

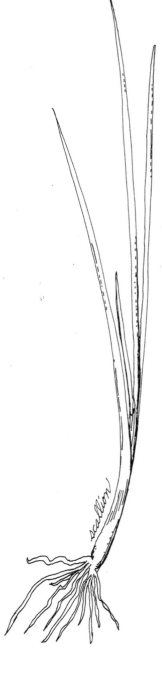

scallion

September

Harvest:
   Swiss chard, parsley,
   tomatoes, carrots,
   bush beans,
   endive, arugula,
   leaf lettuce, bibb lettuce.

October

*Plant outdoors (about October 15
or later)*
   Group C: garlic.
Harvest:
   Swiss chard, parsley,
   tomatoes, endive,
   arugula, leaf lettuce
   bibb lettuce,
   carrots, broccoli.

November

Harvest:
   Swiss chard, parsley,
   broccoli, carrots,
   endive, arugula,
   leaf lettuce, bibb lettuce.
   Also stored
   green tomatoes
   that have turned red.

December

*If you haven't finished shutting
everything down in November, do
it now, as soon as practical!*
   The beds under their cozy
   blankets of shredded leaves
   will get a good sleep and be in
   great shape for next season.
      *Time to relax so that you
too will be in great shape for
next season.*

arugula

11

Saving seed

Seed is expensive. Since one of the tenets of the modular garden is cost effectiveness, saving seed certainly should be considered. Besides saving money there are other good reasons to do so. If you start seed saving now, in just a few years you will have developed plants that are customized for your garden. They will be far superior to any of the seeds available on the market.

Don't be put off by the mystique that has been built up as to the collection of seeds. All you need to know is some basics, take a little care, and simply allow the plants to go to seed. What's more, the seeds from many of the vegetables grown can be had by merely making a few minor changes in the gardening procedures.

Some very basic fundamentals
If you want seed from your vegetables, all you have to do is to let the plants stand long enough to produce them. This is a natural happening and does not need your help. Nonetheless there are certain precautions and steps that should be followed if you are to end up with good viable seed.

Flowering plants produce seed through a process called pollination. The male part of a flower produces pollen that, when it reaches the female part of a flower, begins a chain of events that eventually produces a seed.

Some plants self-pollinate, which means that this process takes place within each flower. Usually no pollen goes from one flower to another, on the same plant or between plants. These plants have what are called "perfect flowers," having both male and female parts. No outside help is needed to produce seed.

Some plants cross-pollinate, which means that pollen is transferred from one flower to another, on the same plant or to others. Generally they have "imperfect flowers." An imperfect flower is either a male, producing only pollen, or a female that produces only seed.

Plants with imperfect flowers can be divided into two categories: 1) Those that have both separate male and female flowers on the same plant, and 2) Those whose entire individual plants are either male or female. That is, plants that have only male flowers, and plants that have only female flowers.

Pollen is spread by the wind or by insects, usually bees. If more than one variety of a vegetable is grown, care must be taken, as one cross-pollinated variety can cross with a different variety of the same species. Normally such plants need to be isolated from other varieties in distance or in time.

In a small garden isolating by adequate distance is difficult or unachievable. So when that is not possible, the choices are: 1) Plant only one variety of a cross-pollinator, or 2) Separate by time.

Since most seeds are viable for more than one year, the danger of cross-pollination between different varieties can be reduced by letting only one, or two, if widely spaced, of each variety go to seed per year, rotating on a yearly basis. In fact, you don't need to save seeds every year. Some years seed saving could be reduced to just a few, or no plants.

As for the self-pollinated plants, ordinarily they can be planted fairly close to different varieties of the same plant without concern regarding unwanted crossings. However, it can happen. Therefore it is best to treat them almost the same way as the cross-pollinators.

When calculating isolation distances between cross-pollinating crops, don't forget to take into consideration any crops that may be growing in nearby gardens. Any walls, solid fences, or high hedges between these gardens and yours will lessen the chances of crossing but not eliminate the possibility.

One precaution: Avoid hybrids for seed saving. Hybrids are a cross between two genetically distinct parents and their offspring

133

will not be uniform. Use open-pollinated, also called standard, varieties for seed saving purposes.
All of the vegetable varieties that I have recommended are of the open-pollinated type.

Some general guidelines for saving seed

Different seeds, having their own individual characteristics, require different gathering and processing methods. However, there are certain principals that can be applied to all.

1) Always choose the healthiest, most productive, earliest fruit bearing, or latest-bolting leaf vegetable, disease-free plants.

2) Generally, seeds should be saved from several individual plants and all mixed together, even if only a small amount is needed. This will give a wider genetic variability.

3) Seed must be mature in order to keep and germinate successfully. If there is risk of losing seed before it is fully ripe, cut the seed stalks and place them, flowerhead down, in paper bags. Store away from direct sun in a dry airy place. (Large brown-paper grocery bags are perfect for this.)

4) All seeds must be thoroughly dry. After gathering them, put in a warm airy place for a week. Remember, seeds must be dry and cool to keep well. Dampness is their worst enemy.

5) Seeds may have bits of dried plant material sticking to them. Some of this can be removed by hand. Seed can also be cleaned by pouring back and forth from one container to another, by running through a kitchen sieve, or just by placing them on a paper towel and gently blowing the debris away. But seed does not have to be perfectly clean, it won't affect germination.

6) Store seeds in small envelopes marked with date and the variety name. Small $3\frac{5}{8}$- by $6\frac{1}{2}$-inch mailing envelopes are perfect for small seeds such as lettuce. Larger envelopes, the $4\frac{1}{8}$- by $9\frac{1}{2}$-inch business size are good for larger seeds such as peas or beans. Keep in cookie tins or jars in a cool dark place.

7) To test viability, about a month before the planting date, put 10 seeds in a warm moist paper towel. After three weeks, at least 5 seeds should have germinated. If not, discard the seed.

Some plants are very easy to collect seed from, others are not. It will take a little time and experimentation before you know which seeds are easy to collect. Start with the easy ones.

Vegetables for seed saving

Beans and peas (self-pollinated—but can cross, especially favas). They are without a doubt the easiest. All that has to be done is to let the pods mature on the vine. When they are dry and papery and the seeds inside hard (should not be easily dented with a thumbnail), they are ready to be collected.

It is best if they are left on the plant to reach this state, but almost dry pods can be harvested and brought inside to finish drying if necessary. The dry, papery pods should be shelled, the hard seeds air dried in a warm place for a few days. After that, pick out the best-looking seeds, put them in paper envelopes, and store.

To save seed with a minimum of disruption to the gardening routine, a bit of improvising will be necessary.

For fava beans and peas this means letting selected plants stand as long as possible. When space is needed for the succession plantings, pull up entire plants and hang upside down outdoors or indoors until ready, then process as described. (Fava bean pods will turn black when seed is ready.)

For bush beans, since no succession planting follows the main crop, just let selected plants stand until fully mature. If you get impatient and want to start winter preparation of the plot, when the thumbnail test leaves only a slight dent, pull and store until completely dry.

Tomatoes (self-pollinated). No deviation from the norm is required, simply select tomatoes from several of the best plants of each variety. Allow them to become very ripe, but not yet rotting. Pick the fruits, cut in half; squeeze out the seeds, pulp and juice into a jar. Add an equal amount of water.

Keep at room temperature for three days to ferment. Stir at least once a day. Good seed will settle on the bottom. After the three days, when you see bubbles rising up or when a layer of mold covers the surface, they're "done."

Add water equal to the amount of the mixture, stir briskly, let settle, pour off the scum and any seeds floating on top. Retain the seeds on the bottom; be careful not to pour them out. Keep repeating this procedure until only clean seeds on the bottom remain. Next pour into a sieve. Wash under running water, lightly rubbing seeds against mesh to remove any gel that remains. Wipe bottom of strainer with a paper towel and empty out on a dish. Then set it in a warm dry place, with good air flow, out of direct sunlight for several days. Stir often to prevent bunching up. When thoroughly dry put seeds in labeled envelopes and store.

Swiss chard (cross-pollinated). Let several plants that overwintered stand so that good cross fertilization will take place. When plants begin to die, collect the seed clusters by cutting off the tops and further dry, head down, in paper bags. When clusters are thoroughly dry and brittle, strip off the seeds, roll to break open. There will be 3 to 5 seeds per cluster. Store.

Parsley (cross-pollinated). Let several overwintered plants stand. Seed is ready when brown and papery. You don't have to wait until they are thoroughly dry. As soon as the stems of the plant look dry and seeds have a brown coat, cut the entire seed head and store it in a paper bag. If held in a dry place for 2 or 3 weeks, the seed can be shaken out of the stalks and stored.

Lettuce (self-pollinated). Lettuces do cross. To guard against this, alternate saving seed of different varieties. For the spring planting, one year allow just the leaf lettuce to bolt to seed. The next year allow only the bibb lettuce to go to seed.

Since the seed is viable for 3 years (sometimes longer), this procedure is practical. In all cases, select plants that bolt last. Let three of each variety bolt to seed.

Seed is ready to harvest when plants begin to yellow and flowerheads develop little fluffs around them, like dandelions. When about 50 percent of flowers have these fluffs, cut off flowerheads with as much stalk as possible and put head down into a large paper bag.

Let seed mature about a month, then shake heads in the bag to separate any remaining seeds from seed heads. Make sure they are thoroughly dry, separate from "fluff," and put into labeled envelopes. As for the fall lettuce, it will not have had the proper conditions to make seed. Any produced will be of poor quality.

Arugula and endive: Collect seed from the spring sowing only. For this sowing, modify harvesting method. Use cut-and-come-again method on nurse rows only. Let plants in main row mature and go to seed.

Arugula (cross-pollinated). Bolts early and will have been harvested for seed before it is time for the succession planting. Just let at least three plants stand for good cross-pollination.

Endive (self-pollinated) is a biennial. But if you sow it very early, it will be exposed to cold and short days that will cause it to produce seed the first year. It can stand in place until the end of the season if the bush beans are just sown around it.

Both arugula and endive are harvested for seed in much the same way. When pods begin to turn from green to brown, harvest all. If not collected at this point, seed pods will burst when ripe and scatter all over the garden. Cut off seed heads and place headfirst in paper bags. When completely dry, crush pods between thumb and fingers; seeds will fall into bag. Seed is very fine; separate from debris by running through a sieve. Allow to dry thoroughly before storing.

Radish (cross-pollinated). When sowing fava beans, radishes are intercropped between the bean plants of the first three, and the last three rows. Let selected plants from the very first and the very last row stand for seed. Several plants are needed for transfer of pollen. Different varieties will cross-pollinate.

To be safe, alternate the variety of these "seed row" plantings from year to year. Seed is viable for about 5 years. Seed is ready when pods turn yellow-brown and are dry. Cut off pods, place in a brown paper bag, and put in a dry place away from heat or sun. In about four weeks the seeds will be ready to remove from the pods. Split open the pods and pick out seeds.

Miscellaneous

Beets, carrots and onions are all biennials. Seed is obtained by either of two ways. 1) They are dug up in the fall and the best ones are chosen, stored, and then replanted the next spring, 2) Overwintered in place and allowed to go to seed the following season.

Broccoli goes to seed in the second year, but there are short season types that if planted very early will go to seed in one year.

Unlike annuals, seed saving from the above cannot be easily incorporated into the normal routine. As with Swiss chard and parsley, special steps need to be taken if their seed is wanted.

Unless you love problems, stick to annuals for seed saving.

Garlic is not grown from seed. For propagating, individual cloves have to be saved and replanted. At harvest time put aside the best bulbs. After drying out with the rest of the crop keep them hung up by their tops, until their late fall planting time.

12

Pest Control

The pests that a backyard gardener has to be concerned with can be put into two categories: 1) Animals and Birds. 2) Bugs and Slugs. In my garden I have had to go to greater lengths to control the animal and bird pests than the bugs and slugs.

There is nothing more frustrating than, after spending several hours painstakingly sowing a crop, to wake up the next morning to find the seedbed dug up and in total disarray. Without effective animal and bird controls this can happen all too often. It was apparent, early on, that the success of my garden depended to a large extent on how successfully these lovable but vexing creatures could be constrained.

On the other hand, the bugs and slugs were a relatively minor inconvenience. Being in the habit of inspecting my crops on a regular basis, it was mostly a question of hand picking or washing off some insect pests with a few squirts of water. This just became a part of my regular routine, and bugs and slugs never became a problem of any significance.

The animal and bird dilemma being number one, as far as I am concerned, it will be the first topic to be discussed.

Animals and Birds
Living in a populated area as I do, there is no problem with real wildlife. My number one enemy is squirrels, who, for reasons known only to themselves, love to romp and dig in spongy soil. My number two enemy is the cat. As soon as a cat discovers a

nice soft piece of earth, that spot becomes its litter box. Birds, at times, are enemies because they consider seeds their rightful meals and can really mess up a sowing. At other times they are my friends as they can eat a lot of bugs.

Many gardening books give "magic" formulas for controlling garden pests. Books state that by using everything from cayenne pepper to mothballs these intruders will keep their distance. If it were only that simple! I have tried most of these "miracle methods," plus a few of my own, without success.

It has been my experience that only a <u>mechanical barrier</u> will protect a garden. This presented a problem, as in my backyard it is not practical or desirable to fence off the entire garden.

Further a fence does not protect newly seeded plots from the birds. I concluded that the solution was to find a way to protect each individual module with its own barrier.

This was accomplished by developing two items. One was what I call a "<u>pest panel</u>," the other, a "<u>module fence</u>."

Pest panels

The basic barrier constructed was the pest panel. This simple item is my first line of defense against small animals and birds.

These interlopers seem to be particularly attracted to the beds in the spring when the ground has been freshly raked and seeds sown. The use of the pest panels during that phase will see your plots through undamaged.

Beyond that, depending on your particular circumstances, you may, or may not, need to take any further animal and bird pest control measures.

The panels are 2- by 8-foot rectangular frames with 1-inch poultry wire stretched within. The panels are not difficult to make. Materials needed are standard 8-foot lengths of 1x2 furring strips* and 2-foot-wide rolls of 1-inch poultry wire (buy vinyl covered if it is available).

These materials are readily available at home improvement centers, lumber yards, and many hardware stores.

Note: Furring strips are specified because they are cheap. Regular 1x2 lumber can be used instead. It will cost more but will give you a better job. Also: Standard size 8-foot-length lumber is sometimes a little longer than 8 feet. If excessive, trim as needed.

A pest panel is made using 1x2 furring strips for the frame. Two 8-foot lengths form the sides, and two 2-foot lengths make the end pieces. Place the two 8-foot lengths parallel on a flat surface 2 feet apart, outside edge to outside edge. Cut two 2-foot end pieces and place one at each end on top of the side pieces to form a rectangle. Attach them using two $1\frac{1}{4}$-inch #6 deck screws at each corner.

Turn the frame over, <u>end pieces facing down,</u> and roll the 2-foot-wide-1-inch poultry wire across lengthwise. Nail down using $\frac{3}{4}$-inch galvanized poultry staples, cut to fit. This finishes one panel. Two panels are needed for each module, as they are used side by side.

The panels are a convenient size, can be handled easily, and are used in a variety of ways:

1) Ground Guard. When beds are bare the pest panels are put down, side by side, right on top of the module directly in contact with the ground. This will prevent squirrels, cats or any other small animals from digging it up.

2) Mulch Maintainer. When beds are mulched in the fall pest panels are put down, side by side, directly on top of the mulch. This keeps the shredded leaf mulch in place, preventing it from being blown away or otherwise scattered.

3) Seedling Shelter. When a bed is freshly sown in the spring, again to protect from small animals and birds, the panels are used. But, in this situation, an extra step must be taken.

The panels have to be raised slightly to allow for the newly germinated seedlings to grow. Simple "I-beams" will have to be constructed. To make an I-beam, cut one $46\frac{1}{2}$-inch length and two $4\frac{3}{4}$-inch lengths of 1x2 furring strip. Using $1\frac{1}{4}$-inch #6 deck screws, attach the $4\frac{3}{4}$-inch pieces, centered, to both ends of the $46\frac{1}{2}$-inch length to form an "I" shape.

Three are needed: One at each end, just within the ends of the frame and one in a central position, between rows. The panels are then placed on their tops, poultry wire side down. Space underneath may seem excessively small, but it isn't, if any larger, squirrels can crawl under and create havoc.

When the seeds have germinated and seedlings have grown to the point that they begin to touch the poultry wire, the panels will have to be removed. At this point, since there is no longer any

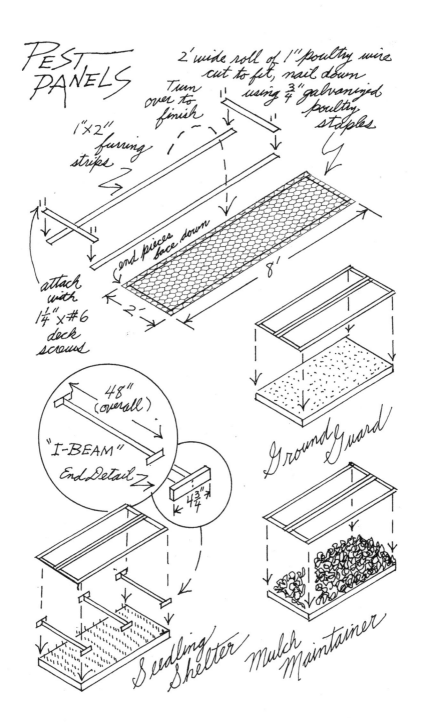

PEST PANELS

2' wide roll of 1" poultry wire cut to fit, nail down using ¾" galvanized poultry staples

Turn over to finish

1"x2" furring strips

end pieces face down

attach with 1¼"x#6 deck screws

8'

2'

48" (overall)

"I-BEAM" End Detail

4¾"

Ground Guard

Seedling Shelter

Mulch Maintainer

141

seed, birds should cease to be a problem and the animal pests may have lost interest. If your pest problem is not too severe, this early season protection may be all that is necessary. Conversely, if there are rabbits or other crop eaters of their kind around you will probably have to go to the next step in the modular pest control system: the erecting of a <u>module fence</u>.

Module fence

The module fence will afford further protection for the plants beyond the seedling stage. While the protection is not total, it is very substantial.

To form a module fence two "<u>end panels</u>" have to be constructed. They are 2- by 4-foot rectangular frames covered with poultry wire. Positioned one at each end of the module, panels are held erect by two posts that are pushed into the ground.

Pest panels are then placed between these end panels in an upright position enclosing the entire module in a mini-fence. The pest panels are held in place by latches and are easily removed when the crops need tending or harvesting, then replaced.

<u>To construct an end panel:</u> All components are cut from standard 8-foot lengths of 1x2 furring strips. Two end panels are needed for each module fence. First, cut two 32-inch strips and saw a point on one end of each (we will call these "<u>posts</u>"). Next, on a flat surface, place two 48-inch strips parallel to each other and 24 inches apart, outside edge to outside edge.

Measure in $1\frac{3}{4}$ inches from each end of the strips and make a vertical pencil mark. Place the 32-inch posts vertically on the 48 inch strips so that both outside edges are on the pencil marks and the flat end is flush on top. The pointed end will extend considerably beyond the lower strip.

On the lower strip only, behind the posts, put $\frac{1}{8}$-inch thick $1\frac{1}{2}$-inch-square shims. (Shims can be cut from plastic detergent jugs; two stacked are about $\frac{1}{8}$ inch thick.) Tack all into position using 4D $1\frac{1}{2}$-inch finishing nails. Check to make sure that all is correct then fasten everything using $1\frac{1}{4}$-inch #6 deck screws.

For the inside top, cut a $44\frac{1}{2}$-inch strip of 1x2. Place so that each end is resting on a post, flush with top and outside edge. Slide shims in between. Attach, then measure in $\frac{1}{4}$ inch from the ends, centered top to bottom, and drill a $\frac{1}{16}$-inch hole. Next, take

END PANEL

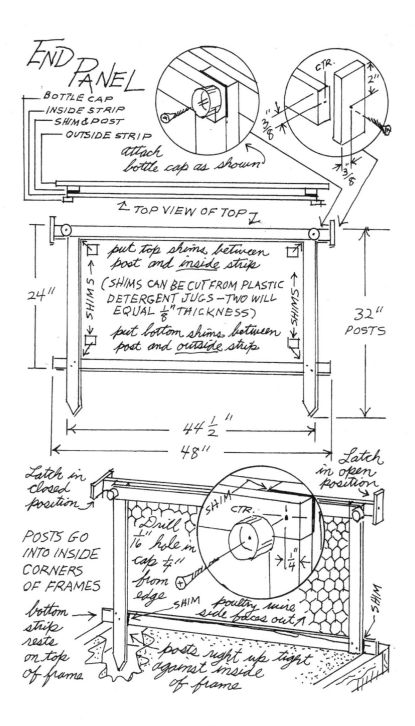

- BOTTLE CAP
- INSIDE STRIP
- SHIM & POST
- OUTSIDE STRIP

attach bottle cap as shown

CTR.

2"

3/8

3/8

↗ TOP VIEW OF TOP ↖

put top shims between post and _inside_ strip

(SHIMS CAN BE CUT FROM PLASTIC DETERGENT JUGS—TWO WILL EQUAL $\frac{1}{8}$" THICKNESS)

put bottom shims between post and _outside_ strip

24"

SHIMS → ↓

← SHIMS

32" POSTS

$44\frac{1}{2}$"

48"

Latch in closed position ↗

Latch in open position ↖

POSTS GO INTO INSIDE CORNERS OF FRAMES

Drill $\frac{1}{16}$" hole in cap $\frac{1}{4}$" from edge

SHIM   CTR.

$\frac{1}{4}$"

SHIM

SHIM

poultry wire side faces out ↗

bottom strip rests on top of frame

posts right up tight against inside of frame

143

a screw-on soda bottle cap (caps are about $1\frac{1}{8}$ inches in diameter), $\frac{1}{4}$ inch from its edge, drill a $\frac{1}{16}$-inch hole. From the inside start a 6 x $\frac{3}{4}$-inch wood screw until its tip protrudes slightly. Line up tip with predrilled hole in top strip and fasten so that biggest part of the cap protrudes beyond the edge. Repeat on the other end. Turn the entire framework over, spread 2-foot-wide-1-inch poultry wire across and nail down using $\frac{3}{4}$-inch poultry staples. Cut to fit.

Last, make latches, two per end panel. Cut a 4-inch piece. In the exact center of the wide dimension, measure in $\frac{3}{8}$ inch from one edge and drill a $\frac{1}{8}$-inch hole. On tip of end panel top 48-inch horizontal strip, also drill a $\frac{1}{8}$-inch hole. This hole should be $\frac{3}{8}$ inch down from the top, centered left to right. Then, using a $1\frac{5}{8}$-inch #6 deck screw, drive it through the predrilled hole of the latch, letting it protrude slightly. Line it up with the predrilled hold on the tip and finish driving the screw to attach.

Repeat on the other side. This will complete one end panel. Two are needed to create a module fence. (See illustration, page 143.)

Erecting the module fence: To assemble a module fence you will need two end panels and two pest panels. The end panels are put up first. At one end of the module, position an end panel so that its poultry wire side is facing out and its posts are at the inside corners of the module frame. Making sure that the posts are right up tight up against the inside of the frame push it down into the soil until the bottom strip of the end panel rests on the frame's top. (If your soil is hard you may not be able to push the posts in. If this is the case, with a trowel dig holes for the posts.) Repeat the same procedure to erect the other panel.

Once the end panels are up, first turn the latches to their open positions. Then place a pest panel, poultry wire side facing out, in between the protruding tips of the end panels. One long rail of the pest panel should be resting on the top of the module frame, both short rails up against the end panel posts. When fully in position, swivel the latches to hold in place. Do the same on the other side. This completes the assembly.

Accessing the module fence: When access is needed, just turn the latches to the open position and lift out the pest panel: It then can be leaned up against one of the end panels for support while you go about your chores. When finished, put the pest panel back in place and turn the latch to the lock position.

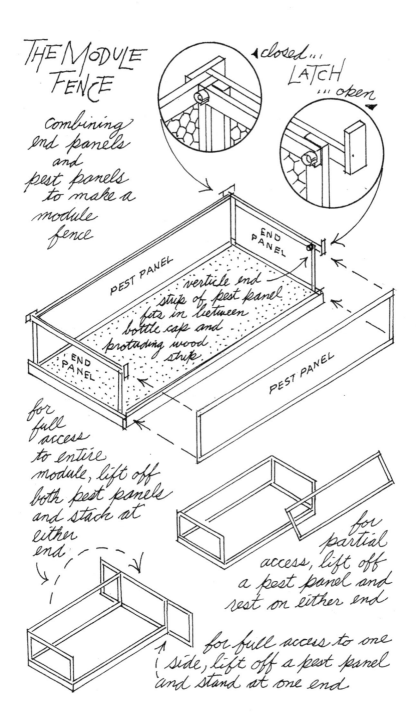

THE MODULE FENCE

combining
end panels
and
pest panels
to make a
module
fence

closed... **LATCH** ...open

END PANEL

END PANEL

PEST PANEL

vertical end
strip of pest panel
fits in between
bottle cap and
protuding wood
strip.

PEST PANEL

for
full
access
to entire
module, lift off
both pest panels
and stack at
either
end

for
partial
access, lift off
a pest panel and
rest on either end

for full access to one
side, lift off a pest panel
and stand at one end

When partial access to the bed is needed, just lift out the pest panel and move it so that it clears your working area. Lean it up against the side of an end panel for support.

When full access to only one side of the bed is needed, lift out that pest panel and carry it to one end of the module and set it down, face to face, leaning it against the end panel.

When full access to the complete bed is needed, remove both pest panels and stand together at one end leaning them slightly against the end panel.

The module fence is a bit of an inconvenience, but it in no way interferes with any of the gardening chores, as it is easily accessed. It should protect from most of the animal pests. Birds, of course, can fly in. But at this stage of the crops' growth, they usually do no damage, just eat a few bugs or grubs, and fly out.

In most situations this should give adequate protection. But if there are still a few unwanted bird or animal interlopers getting in, then the last line of defense is to put on a top.

Topping out

The module fence with a top provides maximum security. Of course the tops can be kept on only as long as the crops within do not get any taller than two feet. For the C group leaf and root crops this is for their full life. For others it will be for a large portion of their growing period.

Pest panels are used as tops, two per module fence. Before making any new ones, analyze your situation, usually there is only one crop group at a time that will need a top. Perhaps freed up panels can be used, or only one new set will be needed.

To put on tops: Simply place two pest panels side by side, poultry wire side down, on top of the module fence so that their ends rest on the end panels. That's all there is to it!

Beyond pest control: The module fence with the top can also be used in cool or hot weather as follows:

1) In early spring, or late fall, it can be covered with clear plastic to provide a warmer mini-climate.

2) In hot weather lath panels can be placed on top to give partial shade to cool season crops. When summer sowing fall crops, it can be covered over with any material to provide full shade, until seeds germinate.

PUTTING ON A TOP

Simply place two pest panels side by side, poultry wire side down, on top of the module fence

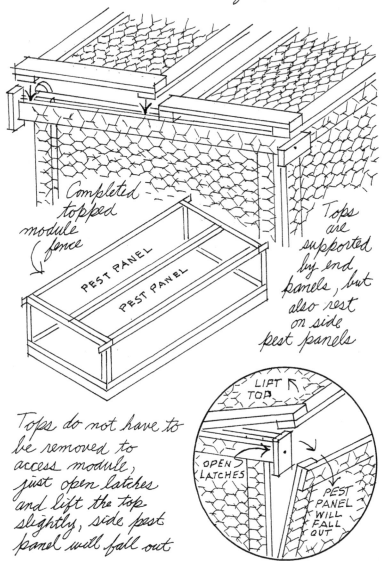

Completed topped module fence

PEST PANEL

PEST PANEL

Tops are supported by end panels, but also rest on side pest panels

Tops do not have to be removed to access module, just open latches and lift the top slightly, side pest panel will fall out

LIFT TOP

OPEN LATCHES

PEST PANEL WILL FALL OUT

Bugs and Slugs

It isn't possible to get rid of all of the insects and the countless other creepy-crawly things that are in a garden, and you shouldn't try to do it. The bug that you hate may be the food supply of a bug you love. Insects are an essential part of nature and will always be there. One has to be tolerant and recognize that all of them are a part of an extremely complicated ecosystem. If you meddle too much you risk throwing it out of balance.

Accordingly, for the home garden there is no question in my mind that we follow nature's way as far as it is practical. This does require a little bit of patience as it will not give you instant results. However, it will give you long-term permanent results.

Short term, if you experience a bug problem, you will have to resist the temptation to buy a pesticide and start spraying everything in sight. If you are starting a new garden using the organic method usually this will not be the case.

If you already have a garden and have been using chemicals, stop! Please don't panic when you see the bugs, upon coming out of their drunken trance, attacking the plants vigorously.

Happily, this situation will be brief, as things will quickly begin to stabilize. Good bugs will start to increase along with the nasty ones, and when they have to cope with more predators and a reduced food supply, a lot of them will die or just leave and everything will revert back to a more natural state.

Once you stop using chemicals, never, never, go back to using them, not even for a one-shot occasion. To do so will set back some of the advances you have achieved.

In the organic garden practice, ongoing control. Routinely inspect your plants, hand-picking the bigger insect pests and washing off smaller ones with a spray of plain water. But, if you see a lady beetle in the midst of a group of aphids do not interfere with her dinner. Leave enough aphids so that she has a food supply. If she runs out of food she will leave your garden.

Cultural controls, the first line of defense

If sound gardening procedures are meticulously followed there is very little chance of having any major pest problems. Briefly, to review the basics of cultural control:

Build up your soil organically. A healthy soil supports a wide range of organisms in providing good growing conditions. This not only lessens the chance of diseases but actually helps control some pests. Healthy plants are not much bothered by a few bugs chewing on their leaves.

Avoid monoculture. A mixed planting creates a more balanced bionetwork that is attractive to beneficial insects. It does not attract an inordinate amount of any one particular type of pest. A variety will be the norm.

Practice good garden hygiene. Remove yellowed wilted leaves from plants. Pick up dropped dead leaves and fruits.

Clean up thoroughly in the fall. Clear and cultivate empty plots to expose larvae.

Mulch the modules for the winter. This will ensure that the beneficial undersoil life will survive through the cold weather.

Rotate crops. Don't forget to move crop groups to a different module every year.

Identify and control, the next step
Beyond cultural controls the next step is to control without doing undue damage. This can be done by using mild sprays and hand-picking. Many household products come in hand-operated plastic spray bottles that can be adjusted to a spray or to a stream. Just wash them out and fill with your own mixture.

I use two of them. One is filled with plain water, the second is filled with a water/soap mixture ($\frac{1}{2}$ teaspoon of Ivory liquid dishwashing soap to a quart of water). When I have an aphid problem, first I try to wash them off using the bottle of plain water adjusted to a stream. If that doesn't work, I go to the second with the mixture.

The following are some of the most common pests you are most likely to encounter:

Black aphids: Small and pear-shaped, they suck juices from tender young growth of fava beans. Clusters of feeding aphids cause stunting and deformation of stems and leaves. Look for them on the new growth at the end of stems. Control by grasping the stem that they are on between the thumb and first two fingers and gently rub back and forth to squash them. Leave the dead aphids on the plant as a deterrent. If this method is used as soon as they first appear, they should not become a problem. Another method used is spraying with the water/soap mixture. However, be aware that this will cause a certain amount of burn on the leaves. Also the infestation will be lessened by pinching off the centers of plants when about 24 inches high. The aphids don't like the rest of the plant as much, because it is bitter. Inspect daily.

Cutworms: Brown, gray, or black caterpillars. Are called cutworms since they sever plant stems. They curl around the base of young stems, chewing through transplants and seedlings near the soil line. Work at night. A real danger to tomato transplants. Controlled by encircling stems with 3-inch-high light cardboard collars. Press into soil around stem at ground level, 1 inch into soil, 2 inches above. The cardboard from cereal boxes is ideal for making these collars.

Leafminers: Most leafminers found on vegetable plants are fly maggots. The parent lays white eggs on leaf undersides. Within four days tiny pale green maggots emerge and start tunneling through the small, microscopic space between the upper and lower top and bottom of a leaf. As feeding continues, the tunnels join together, making light-colored blotches.

Maggots can move from leaf to leaf. They do not do a lot of harm to established plants. Usually attracted to Swiss chard and beets. Just cut out the damaged portions of the leaves, completely remove and destroy badly affected leaves. After three weeks they drop from the plants and spin cocoons in the soil, from which adult flies emerge.

Cultivating under the plants will destroy these maggots, thereby controlling somewhat. Although most leafminers are fly maggots, some are tiny caterpillars or beetle grubs. Cabbage, tomato, pepper, and others may be attacked.

Mexican bean beetle: Adults are tan, round backed, about ¼ inch long with 16 black spots. (Do not confuse with the beneficial lady beetle, which is red with any number of spots.) They hibernate in wooded areas or garden debris. In spring, they fly to bean plants and lay clusters of bright yellow eggs on the undersides of leaves, which develop into yellowish orange larvae.

There can be up to three generations per year. Adults and larvae are plant-feeders. They skeletonize leaves and chew holes in stems and pods. Control by inspecting plants daily. Look for holes eaten in the leaves. Turn over and if any eggs or larvae are

COMMON PESTS

Aphid They come in all colors, green, black, brown or reddish. Pear shaped insect $\frac{1}{16}$" to $\frac{5}{16}$" in length

SHOWN IN ENLARGED SIZE

Cutworm
Brown, gray or black. Works at night. Protect tomato seedlings with stiff paper collars

Leafminer
Very tiny, work within upper and lower leaf top and bottom. Make meandering white or yellow tunnels or papery blotches on leaves

Mexican Bean Beetle
Tan, round backed about $\frac{1}{4}$" long Has 16 black spots

SHOWN IN ENLARGED SIZE

Tomato Hornworm
Dark green with white stripes 3" to 4" in length If not controlled can quickly skeletonize a plant

Slugs
Gray, tan or black. Slimy. Can be anywhere from $\frac{1}{4}$" to 6" or more in length

present, fold the leaf over them and crush them. Hand-pick adults that are found both on top or bottom of leaves.

Tomato hornworm: Green with white stripes, they are about 3 to 4 inches long. Eggs are round yellow-green and can be found on undersides of leaves. Worms are difficult to see, green in color, and are perfectly camouflaged on tomato vines. They do most of their feeding at night. In the morning look for small, black droppings on tops of leaves or on soil under plant. Hornworm usually is somewhere directly above these droppings.

Control by hand-picking. If worm has numerous white cocoons on its back, leave it; these are wasp larvae that will kill it and grow up to infect other hornworms. Any worms that are missed will in time drop to the ground and burrow to pupate. In the spring they will emerge as mature moths and lay eggs on your new plants. The eggs then develop into hungry hornworms. At season's end, with a rake, give a deep 2-inch cultivation over the entire area. This will destroy any pupae that are in the soil.

Slugs: Gray, tan, or black, slimy and soft-bodied, ¼ inch to 8 inches long. Active at night, leave shiny slimy trails. Will attack almost anything. Eat holes on plants, sometimes defoliating them. They hide during the day. Spread used coffee grounds around plants to protect. Caffeine is toxic to slugs and they don't like to crawl over any coarse material. In addition, traps can be made with boards raised slightly above the soil. They will congregate under them before the sun comes up. Another method is to fill empty tuna cans with beer and set into ground up to the top rim. Slugs are attracted to the beer and fall in. Inspect traps daily.

Green aphids: Small pear-shaped, suck plant juices, causing stunting or deformed leaves. As they feed, they exude a sticky substance called honeydew. Ants that eat the honeydew are often a sign of aphid infestations. Soot mold grows on the honeydew. Aphids pass through stages from nymph to adult, both with and without wings. When they become overcrowded on one plant, they all of a sudden develop wings and fly to another plant. Found on a variety of plants. Look for them in clusters under leaves, on buds and shoots. Wash off with a stream of water.

Other pests: The pests listed here are the usual culprits found in the majority of home gardens. For information on any others I suggest consulting a book on garden pests at your local library.

13

Filling in some blanks

Throughout the previous chapters, in the interest of clarity and simplicity, I have tried to present the basics of establishing, working, and managing the three-module home vegetable garden in a straightforward manner without giving a lot of alternatives or introducing other distractions. In this chapter miscellaneous aspects of significance are discussed.

Different possible arrangements of the modules
In my backyard the modules are lined up side by side. The arrangement described in the preceding chapters is a very compact layout, efficient to work, and saves water. It is the recommended arrangement of the three modules.

However, I understand that all backyards are not the same and that, in some, this side-by-side plan will not be practical or possible. In those cases different possibilities will have to be explored. There are many ways in which the modules can be arranged, depending on the configuration of the space available. If the space is irregular and has spots that do not receive sunshine, a creative solution will have to be arrived at. Perhaps widely separating them or even breaking some in half, tucking a half module here and a half there. Keep in mind that minimum 2-foot pathways must be left between and all around.

The modules might be lined up vertically, fit into a corner with one horizontal and the other two vertical, or vice versa, two horizontal and one vertical. Other possibilities could be to stagger them in a variety of ways, or lay them out in a "T" or "L" shape. They can even be split up into two or three different areas: perhaps two modules in the backyard and one in a smaller side yard, or each in a completely different place.

There are numerous possibilities limited only by a person's imagination. But always keep in mind that a compact layout is easier to maintain.

Since there are probably many possible arrangements that can fit your site, it may be a good idea to do some planning on paper first. Go out and walk around the available space. Notice where the sun shines most of the day, the condition of the soil, where there are trees, fences, or other structures, and where the water source is. You could start by just making some rough freehand sketches to compare different configurations.

Once you narrow down the choices, if you're unsure about everything fitting, a more accurate drawing can be made. Go out and, using a tape measure, measure off key points and mark them on your sketch.

Using this sketch as a starting point, make a more precise sketch, using a scale of $\frac{1}{4}$ inch to 1 foot, and lay out the area on a large piece of paper. Using the same scale, on a smaller piece of paper draw three 1- by 2-inch rectangles. These will represent the three 4- by 8-foot modules. Cut out these rectangles and place them on the scale drawing of the available space. Move them around until they are in the positions that you think best, then paste or tape them down. This will now be your blueprint.

With the sketch as a guide, go out to the actual site and measure out their positions. But before doing any digging, I recommend that you first construct the 4- by 8-foot wood frames. Place them on the ground in the positions indicated on your scale drawing. Then for the next few days, observe the patterns of sunshine and shade. Do they receive enough sun? Are they in a convenient spot? Make sure that they are exactly where you want them before starting the preparation of the beds.

If you're not into drawing sketches, you can skip that step and just make the frames and move them around in the area to determine the best arrangement. You may have to do a lot of lifting and carrying before it's all over, but in the end it allows a precise location of the modules before doing any spade work.

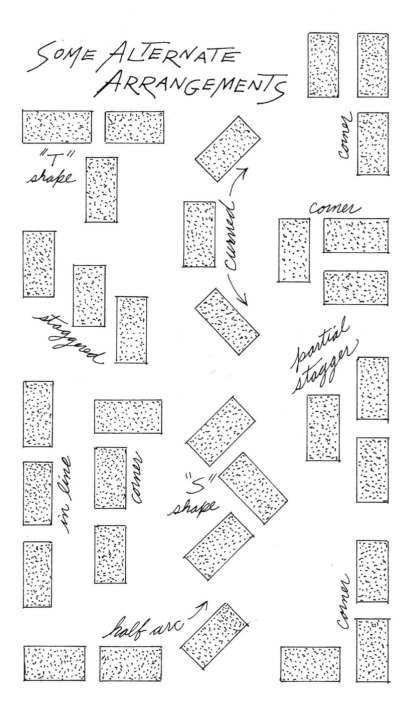

SOME ALTERNATE ARRANGEMENTS

"T" shape

corner

curved

corner

staggered

partial stagger

in line

corner

"S" shape

corner

half arc

Dressing up the modules
Anything done to "fancy up" the looks of the modules is strictly optional. From their inception the modules in my backyard were surrounded by sod and gave an attractive appearance.

But as time went by, grass began creeping under the wood frames and trying to establish itself in the beds. To counteract this, I cleared a narrow strip all around the frames. This strip was kept free of grass and weeds by regular cultivation.

Patio blocks
I was perfectly happy with things as they were. But one day I received a flyer from a local gardening supply store advertising 8x16 patio blocks at a very cheap price. The thought occurred to me that if patio blocks were put down in the bare strips around the frames, the need for cultivating would be eliminated.

That was a practical reason, that the appearance would be improved was secondary. I decided to give it a try. It turned out to be a lot of work and I found that the blocks were not exactly 8 inches x 16 inches as advertised, but slightly undersized.

This was discovered when six 16-inch-long blocks laid end to end came about 2 inches short of 8 feet. The problem was solved by buying 8x8 blocks, cutting them in half, and putting them in the ground edgewise at the center point in the row (blocks are 2 inches thick).

Another decision to be made was whether to butt them up against the outside of the frame or to put them slightly under the frame. The latter was chosen, reasoning that if they butted the frame, over time they would tend to pull away.

Each module requires twenty 8x16 blocks and one 8x8 block (each end taking four 8x16s and each side taking 6 plus the half 8x8). The blocks do give the modules a more finished look and act as mower strips.

Cultivation around the frames is no longer needed, but there is work required to keep the grass from growing over the blocks.

Not intended as a pest control measure, but I suppose that the blocks would deter any small animals from tunneling under the frame to gain access, if stymied by a module fence.

Patio blocks are a nice enhancement but they are strictly an optional "luxury" item.

PATIO BLOCKS

Edging the beds with patio blocks prevents grass from creeping under the frames, acts as mower strips and enhances the appearance of the module

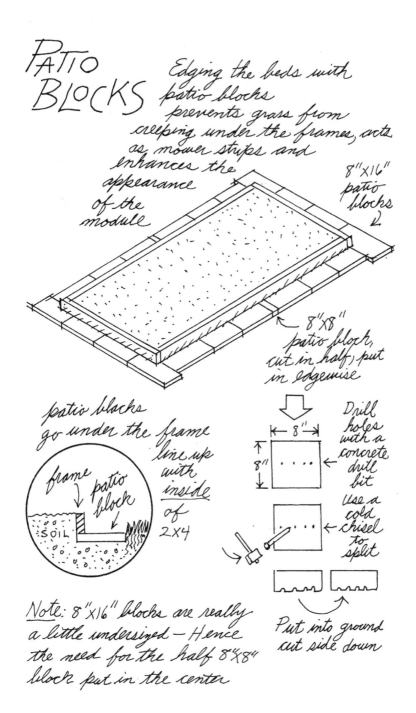

8"X16" patio blocks

8"X8" patio block, cut in half, put in edgewise

patio blocks go under the frame line up with inside of 2X4

frame

patio block

SOIL

8"

8"

Drill holes with a concrete drill bit

Use a cold chisel to split

Put into ground cut side down

Note: 8"X16" blocks are really a little undersized — Hence the need for the half 8"X8" block put in the center

Modular components as possible season extenders

Seeds take a long time to germinate in cold soil. I don't believe in rushing the season, but for those who do, I offer the speculative procedure that is illustrated on the facing page.

As soon as the mulch is removed in the spring, rake the soil and leave it bare for a few days. Then cover the full module with a sheet of clear plastic to trap the heat and warm up the soil.

Place bricks or long lengths of 2x4s on the edges to hold it down. After about a week or so, remove the plastic and sow the seed, water, then put up a seedling shelter. Cover the entire shelter with the clear plastic to create a mini-greenhouse. Hold plastic down as before. The plastic will keep the moisture and heat in, and the cold winds out.

After the seeds have germinated and the seedlings are growing, when it is sunny, to acclimatize, take off the plastic for short periods during the warmest part of the day.

When seedlings start to touch the pest panel poultry wire, everything has to come off. If they still need protection from garden pests, erect a module fence.

If not yet acclimatized, cover with the clear plastic. Continue removing the plastic during the day for increasing longer lengths of time until it can be removed permanently.

At the other end of the season, in the fall, the covered module fence can be used to protect the plants and to keep them producing longer, providing an extended harvest.

Theoretically the above should result in earlier crops. But I have never fully tested this, so there are no promises. Anyone wishing to try this process will have to learn by trial and error.

Modular plant props and lath panels

In a vegetable garden there are always situations where plants need support, containment, or, in hot weather, partial shade.

The plant props and lath panels that I designed for the modular garden will perform all of these functions. As with all the other components, they are modular in form.

They can be used individually or in combinations. Wood laths, usually $1\frac{3}{8}$ inches wide and 4 feet long are used for their construction (some sold are $1\frac{1}{2}$ inches wide). They come in bundles at lumber yards. Quantity in a bundle will vary, usually

STRETCHING THE SEASON

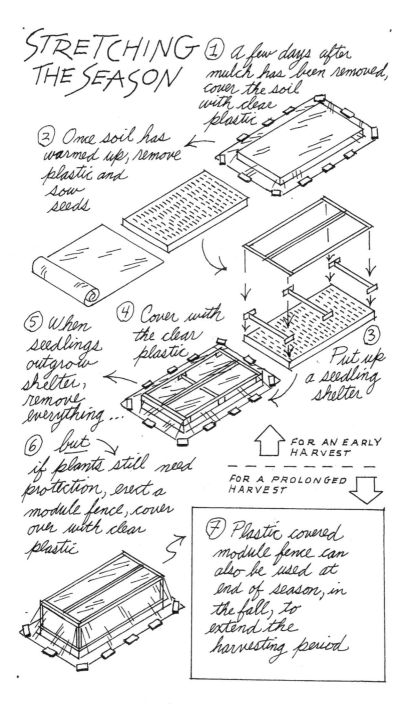

① A few days after mulch has been removed, cover the soil with clear plastic

② Once soil has warmed up, remove plastic and sow seeds

③ Put up a seedling shelter

④ Cover with the clear plastic

⑤ When seedlings outgrow shelter, remove everything...

⑥ but if plants still need protection, erect a module fence, cover over with clear plastic

FOR AN EARLY HARVEST

FOR A PROLONGED HARVEST

⑦ Plastic covered module fence can also be used at end of season, in the fall, to extend the harvesting period about 45, more or less. Being cheap lumber, some will be slightly bent or curved. Use those for the lath panels, a few bent ones put in every other row or so won't really affect the panel. Brush some nontoxic water sealer on all to protect against warping.

Making a plant prop
Pick out laths that are relatively straight. Cut one in half. Make a point on one end of each piece. These will be the upright posts.

Place the two posts on a flat surface 44½ inches apart, outside edge to outside edge. Then position a full lath across, resting on their tops. Both ends of the lath should protrude 1¾ inches.

Tack into position with 1-inch wire nails. Measure down 19 inches from the top, line up the <u>bottom</u> of another lath with this mark, and tack it down. Check that everything is square, then final nail with ¾-inch poultry staples. This will complete the basic plant prop. It will serve to hold tall plants upright when placed next to them. But to control tall leafy plants from flopping over and smothering any low growers next to them, the basic plant prop needs to be modified. Cover with poultry wire by nailing it onto all outside edges of the frame. Bend over any staple tips that go through. Cut to fit. The wire will contain the leafy plants without affecting air circulation. If the plant props are to be used within a module fence, the protruding tips will have to be trimmed ¾ inch, reducing the width to 46½ inches, so that it fits.

Note: *For sturdier props construct using 1x2 furring strips or 1x2 lumber and 1¼-inch #6 deck screws (2 at each corner).*

Making a lath panel
Cut one lath in half for side pieces. On both, marks have to be made to show where cross laths will go. Measure down 1¹⁄₁₆ inch from an end and make a mark that will indicate the position of the <u>top</u> edge of the first cross lath. Then from that point down, make marks at 3-inch intervals all the way to the other end. These designate the positions of the <u>top</u> edge of the other cross laths.

Place these marked pieces on a flat surface 44½ inches apart, outside edge to outside edge. Starting from the first mark, place a lath across the <u>top</u> edge on the mark, to protrude an equal 1¾ inches at both ends. Tack down. On the second mark put down another lath. Tack into position. Continue until all

PLANT PROP

MATERIALS NEEDED FOR BASIC PROP ✱
- Three 1⅜" x 48" wood laths
- ¾" poultry staples

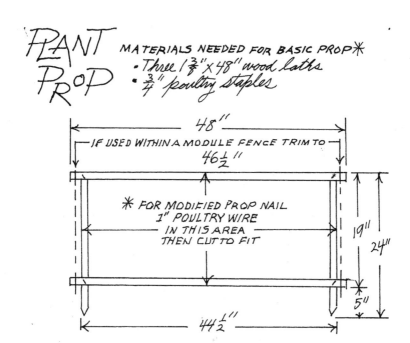

48"

IF USED WITHIN A MODULE FENCE TRIM TO 46½"

✱ FOR MODIFIED PROP NAIL 1" POULTRY WIRE IN THIS AREA THEN CUT TO FIT

19"

24"

5"

44½"

LATH PANEL

MATERIALS NEEDED
- Nine 1⅜" x 48" wood laths
- ¾" poultry staples

3" TOP TO TOP OF LATHS

LATHS 1⅜" WIDE

SPACES BETWEEN LATHS 1⅝"

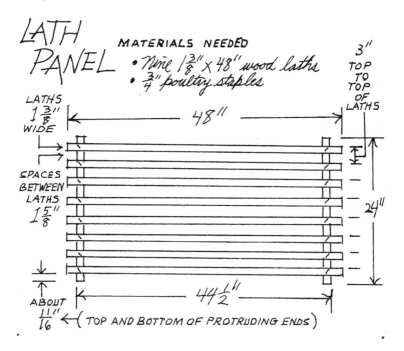

48"

24"

ABOUT 11/16" ← (TOP AND BOTTOM OF PROTRUDING ENDS)

44½"

TYPICAL APPLICATIONS

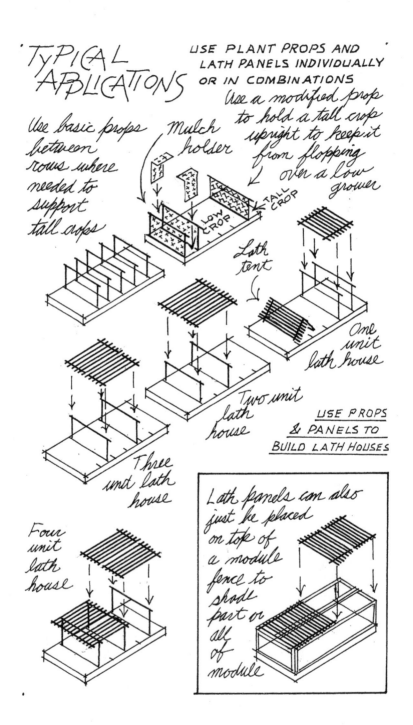

USE PLANT PROPS AND LATH PANELS INDIVIDUALLY OR IN COMBINATIONS

Use basic props between rows where needed to support tall crops

Use a modified prop to hold a tall crop upright to keep it from flopping over a low grower

Mulch holder

LOW CROP

TALL CROP

Lath tent

One unit lath house

Two unit lath house

USE PROPS & PANELS TO BUILD LATH HOUSES

Three unit lath house

Four unit lath house

Lath panels can also just be placed on top of a module fence to shade part or all of module

162

laths are in place, then final nail all using ¾-inch poultry staples. This will complete a lath panel. Four panels will cover a complete module. Make as many as you need.

Typical uses of plant props and lath panels

To contain crops: When a leafy tall crop is dropping over a low grower, place a modified plant crop (one with poultry wire) in between to keep it upright. Push prop in until bottom lath rests on top of the module frame.

Use modified plant props to hold up Swiss chard and parsley winter mulches. If within a module fence, only one is required for each planting unit as there will be support on all sides. Fill up to the 19-inch top with shredded leaves, then cover with plastic.

Two are needed if freestanding—one on both sides of the plants. To close the ends, cut a 16-inch strip from a 2-foot wide roll of 1-inch poultry wire. Fasten to posts with wire ties. Fold down excess at the top. (See illustration on facing page.) Cover the whole thing with plastic, wrap clothesline all around, and tie.

To support tall growers: Crops such as fava beans sometimes need support, especially during very heavy rains that will make them lean over. Basic plant props (or modified props) can be placed between rows wherever needed to keep them upright.

To shelter tomato transplants when hardening off: Lean two lath panels against each other to lock in at the peak. Tie tops together with wire ties. This tent will cut exposure to sun and wind to about half. For added shielding put plants in a cardboard box that is about 6-inches high before putting into the tent.

To give partial shade: Cool season vegetables need protection from the hot sun during warm weather. This can be accomplished by shading with the lath panels in various ways:

1) Freestanding lath houses can be erected in different sizes where needed. Push plant props in until bottom lath rests on top of the module frame. Then place lath panel, or panels, on top to cover the area. (See illustration on facing page.)

2) Lath panels can be put on top of a module fence. Simply place them side by side on the top. Use as many as needed to cover a section or the entire module.

3) Lath tents are a quick easy way to shade newly sown rows in their early stages of growth.

14

Substitutions

The varieties and vegetables grown in the three-module home vegetable garden are the end result of much evaluating.

Varieties used are those that have been proven to be of good quality and are reliable.

Vegetables planted are those that are commonly found in the typical home garden.

That aside, recognizing that every individual has different tastes, preferences, and needs, this chapter attempts to give some guidance in selecting alternatives.

Varietal substitutions

There are many varieties to choose from. However, I can only attest to varieties that I have grown in the past and have found to be satisfactory. Therefore those are the only ones that will be found on the acceptable substitute list. If you are contemplating a variety that is not on the list, it may well be an excellent choice, but before making any substitutions research carefully.

Varieties differ greatly in time of maturity, in quality, and in disease resistance. Success or failure of a crop may be determined by the choice of variety. Try new varieties on a limited scale until they prove themselves.

A word about hybrids

All of the vegetable varieties recommended in this book are of the open-pollinating type (also called standard). If the reader wants to save his own seed, these varieties give the opportunity to do so. Sowing the seeds of hybrids is not recommended as they do not come true. In selecting varietal substitutions, if a person isn't interested in saving seed, then there is no reason why hybrids cannot be picked.

There are a lot of very good hybrids on the market to choose from and they are featured in many seed catalogs.

In the seed industry hybrids are given a designation of "F1." This indicates the first generation after the cross between two different pure varieties. As a result of this cross the ensuing plant has more vigor than either of its parents. The downside is, that since seed saved from F-1 plants will not be uniform, new hybrid seed must be produced each year by repeating this cross.

Commercially grown corn has been one of the greatest beneficiaries of hybridization, producing varieties with larger cobs and bigger sweeter kernels.

Also, some hybrid melons have been bred to ripen much sooner than standard ones. For other crops the results have not been so impressive; some have shown little upgrading.

In any case, I have included a few hybrids that I have grown in the past and was pleased with on the list of acceptable varietal substitutions that follows.

Vegetable and Variety	Acceptable Varietal Substitutes
Arugula *(Herb)*	
Astro	Arugula (Rocket), Arugula (Roquette)
Beets	
Detroit Dark Red	Early Wonder, Firechief, Ruby Queen, Honey Red
Broccoli	
De Cicco	Calabrese, Waltham 29, Packman *(Hybrid)*
Bush Beans	
Bush Blue Lake	Provider, Contender
Carrots	
Royal Chantenay	Danvers, Nantes Half Long
Endive	
Green Curled	Salad King, Frisan

Vegetable and Variety	*Acceptable Varietal Substitutes*
Fava Beans	
Aquadulce...........................	Broad Windsor Long Pod
Garlic *(Herb)*	
Elephant..............................	New York White, German Extra-Hardy
Lettuce	
Buttercrunch.........................	Summer Bibb, Big Boston, Dark Green Boston
Simpson Elite........................	Black-Seeded Simpson, Slo Bolt, Royal Green
Parsley *(Herb)*	
Plain Dark Green Italian............	Gigante d'Italia, Italian Parsley
Onions	
Southport White.....................	White Lisbon, Walla Walla Sweet, White Sweet Spanish
Peas	
Improved Laxton's Progress........	Little Marvel, Frosty, Alaska
Radishes	
Champion.............................	Cherry Belle, Cherriette *(Hybrid)*, French Breakfast
Comet.................................	White Icicle, Sparkler
Swiss Chard	
Rhubarb Chard......................	Lucullus, Bright Lights
Tomatoes	
Delicious.............................	Brandywine, Costoluto Genovese, Better Boy *(Hybrid)*
Earliana..............................	Bonny Best, Anna Russian, Cold Set, Early Girl *(Hybrid)*

You may have difficulty getting some of the varieties listed, as there is a lack of uniformity in names applied to garden vegetables. Sometimes the exact same variety is called different names by different seed companies.

Generally the old tried and true varieties retain their names regardless of who lists them. I would also like to point out that although, for simplicity, I have arugula, parsley, and garlic under the heading of vegetables, they are really herbs. Many seed catalogs have them listed as such. Finally, it is better to order your seeds direct from seed catalogs rather than buying them off the rack at supermarkets, gardening centers, or other stores.

The seed mailed direct from the seed companies has been properly stored under controlled conditions to retain viability. This is not always the case with the seed-rack packets. Temperatures and humidity in retail stores can vary greatly before the packets are sold, which will affect the germination rate of that seed.

Vegetable substitutions

As was stated previously, the crops grown in the three-module home vegetable garden are traditional ones. They are good picks for the average family, but tastes and needs vary greatly. Each person should grow what is best for them.

If changes are desired, they must be thought out carefully. Crops grown in the initial planting should be replaced by comparable vegetables that are suitable to early sowing and have approximately the same maturity dates.

The same applies to succession planting substitutions. Also, crop classification and rotation requirements must be considered.

Review the crop rotation principles carefully before making any final decisions.

Deciding on the changes

For certain substitutions there will be no problems, for example:

To substitute for broccoli, any of the following could be chosen: Brussels sprouts, kohlrabi, kale, or turnips. All are cool weather crops, all are in the *Cruciferae* family, and none will have any effect on the crop rotation sequence.

The same applies if parsley were to be replaced by parsnips. Both are members of the same family, both occupy the ground for the full season, and both can be overwintered and harvested in the following spring.

Also fully compatible in this respect are peppers and eggplant as replacements for some of the tomato plants. Same family, same growing conditions required.

These types of replacements stay within the rotation system and do not require any reevaluating.

167

Beyond those easy changes, one must proceed cautiously. Any other substitutions should be studied and analyzed carefully.

Don't forget the basic principle of not following any crop with another of its family.

To help in this respect, for your reference, common garden vegetable families are listed below:

Family Name	Family Member
Amaryllidaceae	Garlic, leeks, onion, shallot
Chenopodiaceae	Beet, Swiss chard, spinach
Compositae	Globe artichokes, chicory, dandelion, endive, escarole, lettuce, radicchio, salsify
Cruciferae	Arugula, broccoli, Brussels sprouts, cabbage, cauliflower, cress, kale, kohlrabi, mustard greens, radish, rutabaga,turnip
Cucurbitaceae	Cucumber, gourd, melon, pumpkin, summer and winter squashes
Gramineae	Corn
Leguminosae	Bean, lentils, peas, peanuts
Solanaceae	Eggplant, garden huckleberry, ground cherry, pepper, potato, tomato
Umbelliferae	Carrot, celeriac, celery, parsley, parsnip
Valerianaceae	Corn salad

Also, another of the guiding principles to be kept in mind: do not follow a heavy feeder with another heavy feeder. Generally, leaf vegetables and nonlegumes that bear fruits are heavy feeders. Root crops are usually light feeders. Legumes are givers, soil improvers.

Having said all that, grow the vegetables that you like and eat the most. I wouldn't worry too much if your plant cycle does not conform 100 percent to the rotation guidelines.

When it comes to picking an alternate for either a variety or a vegetable, there is such a wide range of choices on the market that one can get very confused.

Talking to other gardeners, getting their advice, and a few samples of their produce, if possible, can be a big help. Beyond that, anything marked "All-America Selections Winner" is a good bet, as this designation indicates that it was chosen in nationwide trials for superior adaptability and vigor for the home garden. In any case, you really won't know for sure how a new selection is going to work out until you actually grow it under your local conditions.

In concluding this discussion on varietal and vegetable substitution I would like to revisit a subject that was previously briefly touched on, but is deserving of a more detailed discussion. That is, the question of seed availability of the selected varieties and vegetables.

Every year, since seed houses can carry only a set amount of cultivars, as new selections are brought out, older ones are dropped. As a result, you may have difficulty finding all of your picks from one source. If buying off the rack, which I do not recommend, one might go from rack to rack at different retail stores and still not find them all.

If buying from seed catalogs, which I strongly advise, if you go through enough of them, I'm sure that you will be able to find most, if not every one. The rub is that all may not be available from one source. If this is the case, then there is a problem. It is economically foolish to split the order between two or more seed companies, as each charges shipping and handling fees. To do so could double or even triple these costs. Therefore it is suggested that all ordering be done from one catalog only.

Pick the one that lists most of the desired varieties and vegetables. Then you will have to ascertain whether you can obtain the missing items from your local seed racks, or just pick substitutes. Usually, the best choice is to pick substitutes. This is not necessarily a bad thing as there are many excellent varieties and vegetables on the market that I have never personally gotten around to and therefore are not mentioned within these pages.

You may find something that suits you just fine.

15

Experimentation

My vegetable garden is a work in progress. Today it is very much different than it was when first started, and in the future I suspect that it probably will be a little different than it is now. As the years go by there are always refinements to be made, new approaches to be discovered.

Changes come about by careful observation, diagnosing the conditions that exist, and deciding if modifications are needed. In gardening altering the status quo takes time, as the results of any experimentation are usually not known until the end of the growing season. Then any subsequent trials have to wait until the following year. This can be overcome, somewhat, by beginning a number of tests all at the same time. In this way one can have the results in one year instead of perhaps four or five years, if done singly.

Your garden is unique—there is no other exactly like it
What grows great in one person's garden does not necessarily do well in another's. Soils, drainage, air circulation, all vary from one location to another. If there is a problem, test—don't guess.

For example: If small seed germination failures are being experienced, tests should be run starting with the sowing process. Very small seed, after being pressed into the earth, can be covered with soil or just left uncovered. To resolve which method results in the best germination rate, one half of the seed sown would be covered, the other half uncovered. Final results would determine if further tests are needed.

This sort of thing goes a long way toward improving one's gardening skills. If you decide to conduct experiments, based on my experience, I can offer the following counsel:

Recognize that no matter how meticulously one formulates a theory, expect the unexpected when the theory is put to the test under actual conditions.

In testing new methods, it is very difficult to remain objective. One wants their brainchild to be successful so badly that there is the tendency to develop a blind spot to any of its shortcomings. Don't let this happen! Admit failures, put them behind you, and build on small successes.

To attain valid results, any test that you do must be performed duplicating scientific methods as much as possible.

Controlled Experiments

There are basically two types of experiments that will give you the answers to most of your questions:

    1) Simple—this is the testing of only one set of variables.

    2) Factorial—this is the testing of more than one set of variables at the same time.

In either case before doing anything, have a clear picture of what it is that you want to accomplish.

Simple Test: Suppose that you want to find out whether bean variety A or bean variety B is more productive under normal conditions. There is only one variable: the different varieties. The procedure would be to do a controlled experiment as follows:

    1) Sow one half of a plot that has normal soil with variety A and the other half with variety B.

    2) Treat both sowings exactly the same, weed, water, and cultivate with no variation.

    3) If at the end of the trial period variety A has produced more beans that B, then it is reasonable to conclude that A is more productive since everything else was the same.

But if one wants to find out about more than one thing, then a factorial test is needed.

Factorial Test: Now suppose you want to know not only whether variety A or variety B is more productive but also how compost or mulch affect the growth of the crops, then it gets a little more complicated.

Controlled Experiments

hypothetical testing of two bean varieties in a module

✓ Simple

testing only one set of variables

To find out:
➤ If variety A or variety B is more productive under normal conditions

} all normal soil

✓ Factorial

testing more than one set of variables

To find out:
➤ If variety A or variety B is more productive
➤ How would compost or mulch affect growth

} normal soil

} heavily composted soil

} mulched soil

A two factor test must be made: The different varieties being one factor and the different soil treatments being the other. Then the procedure would be:

    1) Sow A in one half of a normal soil area.
    2) Sow B in the other half of the normal soil area.
    3) Sow A in one half of a heavily composted area.
    4) Sow B in the other half of the heavily composted area.
    5) Sow A in one half of a mulched area.
    6) Sow B in the other half of the mulched area.

Each soil treatment represents a different approach. The purpose of doing a comparative experiment is to find out if it matters whether one approach is used rather than the other.

At the end of the trial period the results will have to be analyzed. Which variety was the most productive? But why? Did the different soil treatments have anything to do with the results? If yes, it can be assumed that that was an important factor.

Although a factorial test gives more information, it is more complex to set up, carry out, and analyze.

Conducting a test

Start by writing down your objective in a logbook, then record all successive data. In scientific experiments this is to be done by recording in ink in bound notebooks. For your tests this, of course, is not mandatory. But it is still a good idea as it eliminates the temptation to alter entries, or omit pages.

Record everything in the log. Don't just write yourself a note on a scrap piece of paper and please, please don't think that you are going to remember something that you didn't write down!

For my log I use a $9\frac{3}{4}$- by $7\frac{1}{2}$-inch school composition-type bound notebook. The front part is used to record my experiments, the back pages for entering other observations. (Turning the book upside down transforms the last page into page one for that part.)

Most tests can be made with very little change in the normal routine. To illustrate: For years I had been growing bush beans in conventional rows, 2 inches apart in the row, rows 8 inches apart. This usually required some cultivating between rows. I decided to conduct a simple test to determine if sowing them in closer staggered rows would make a difference. A summary follows:

Case history

Title:
Bush beans conventional rows *versus* staggered rows.

Purpose of the test:
To determine if the method of planting has any significant effect on growth and maintenance of bean plants.

Method of conducting test:
1) Four conventional rows filled a marked-off area. Seeds were positioned 2 inches apart in rows 8 inches apart. This resulted in a total of 88 seeds being sown (14 more that the staggered rows).

2) Seven staggered rows filled an identical area. Seeds were positioned 4 inches apart in rows 4 inches apart. This resulted in a total of 74 seeds being sown (14 less than the conventional rows).

3) Both were treated identically. No cultivating was done. They were watered daily until established, then they were watered only if there was no rainfall in any seven-day period.

Monitoring the test:
The plots were checked on a daily basis. After three weeks, the number of seedlings was counted. Staggered rows had a germination rate 4 percent better than the conventional.

It was observed that the exposed bare earth between the conventional rows dried out quickly. This did not happen in the staggered rows. The plants shaded the ground, holding the moisture in. As a result they grew faster and bigger than those in the conventional rows.

Results:
Upon harvesting it was found that the plants in the staggered rows had produced about 10 percent more beans.

Conclusion:
Since the bush beans sown in staggered rows produced more with fewer seeds, retained soil moisture better, and did not need to be cultivated, it was decided to adopt that method for all future sowings.

16

Conclusion

I would like to end this book by going back to some beginnings. In Victory Hill, Pennsylvania, where I grew up, almost everyone had a vegetable garden, their gardening know-how having been passed down from generation to generation. They raised their crops the old-fashioned way, tilling, hoeing, working manure and other organic material into the soil.

Much of what was done then is now incorporated into what is called the "organic method." This system believes in working with nature in the control of garden pests and diseases and in using only organic material to improve the soil. It is a simple and cheap way of growing vegetables.

On the other hand, there are the believers in what is called the "scientific method." This school of thought attempts to control every phase of gardening by man-made chemicals and fertilizers. It is a complex, expensive way of growing vegetables.

The big commercial farmers claim that it is the only way to produce enough food to feed the world's population. Organic gardening experts don't agree. And neither do I!

Organic gardening and the modular system
As a home gardener I have always practiced the organic method as I believe it to be superior to the scientific method. It is an important aspect of my modular garden.

Accordingly, in working the ground its fundamentals should always be kept in mind. Remember that since the basic element necessary for a healthy garden is a healthy plant in healthy soil, all that can be done to improve the soil structure must be done. This means raising the fiber and humus level by systematically adding organic material.

Organic materials are usually livestock manures or compost. For most of us, livestock manure is not available, so compost will have to be the mainstay of a soil-building program.

Organic matter binds soil particles together, provides a spongelike texture that holds moisture for the plants' roots, feeds earthworms, and provides nutrients for the plants.

The shredded leaf mulch put down for the winter not only acts as a soil conditioner but also as a fertilizer. It keeps moisture in, prevents the surface from drying out, and protects the ground from wind and water erosion.

The decay of the leaves on the bottom of the mulch releases nutrients and adds minerals to the soil. Moreover, the mulch allows earthworms and other beneficial bacteria in the soil to survive the winter.

Rotation is essential to growing plants by organic methods as it allows the build-up of nutrients without seriously depleting any particular one.

Different crops require different nutrients. If rotated, no one nutrient is drained. All are used in turn, none too heavily, and the soil remains balanced.

Some thoughts on upsizing the modular garden
The original makeup of my garden was three modules. But during the long process of experimentation and development the number of modules varied from time to time (six at one point).

In the end, to realize the parameters that I had set for myself, the original three-module form was the obvious solution.

To satisfy different parameters the number of modules could be increased without limit. Of course the same basic principles and crop rotation considerations that apply to the three-module form would still have to be applied to any enlarged version.

If one has the space and the energy, modules could be added to grow crops that require a lot of space, such as corn or zucchini. Crops like these would need a full module, or at least a half, to themselves. As modules are added they possibly could be worked into the crop rotation sequence of the existing modules. But, if many are added, a rotation sequence probably would have to be worked out in groups of three or four.

I can easily envision home gardens with nine, twelve, or even fifteen modules. Anything beyond that number pretty much leaves the realm of home gardening and enters the world of the commercial grower.

About garden diaries

This book started out as a simple garden diary. Everybody should consider keeping one. It doesn't have to be elaborate. It can be as uncomplicated as just jotting down comments in a notebook from time to time, or marking planting dates on a calendar. Your personality will dictate what is best for you.

When I first decided to establish a garden in my backyard, I spent a lot of time planning and visualizing its form in my mind.

Then, in order to clarify the details, I began a garden diary by putting thoughts into written words and sketches in a notebook. A garden map was one of the first entries, followed by planting dates and details of the sowings.

As the season went on I inspected my crops on a daily basis, penning in my observations. I also jotted down any other random thoughts that popped into my mind.

At season's end all that had been recorded was summarized. During the winter everything was again reviewed and plans were outlined for the next year. With my diaries it was always possible to look back at previous years to refresh my memory.

The act of writing also puts your mind in a different mode, giving insights into solutions not normally thought of. It forces more thoughtful concentration.

In fact, the process of organizing and rewriting all of those scribblings into book form was instrumental in focusing my thinking and finalizing the form and contents of the three-module home vegetable garden.

Raised-Bed Vegetable Gardening Made Simple was written out of a sincere desire to pass on to others the basics of my modular system plus some of the know-how accumulated during a lifetime of growing vegetables. It is hoped that the reader has benefited—**Good Gardening!**

Appendix

RANDOM RAMBLINGS: TOMATO GROWING NITTY-GRITTY

For those who, for whatever reason, do not want to use the cluster cage system, here are three other methods. Over the years I have used all three with good results—take your pick!

Staking

This is the old tried-and-true method and still used by many home gardeners. A single 6- or 8-foot stake is driven into the ground next to each transplant and the vine is tied to it as it grows. Stakes need to be very sturdy as the plants, when loaded with fruits, will be quite heavy—2- x 2-inch poles are best but 1x2s will do.

To make tying up easier, some gardeners limit growth by pruning suckers and letting only one or two main stems develop. Suckers are shoots that grow out from the stem right above a leaf branch, as shown on page 180.

Caging

Cages keep tomatoes off the ground without the tying. They are made of heavy-duty wire and have large openings so that the tomatoes can be picked easily. They are just put over the plants and the plants grow up into them—a great method! Do not prune.

They should be anchored by driving a stake as tall as the cage into the ground at one side and tying the cage to it.

Those sold are either round or square. You can make your

SUPPORTING THE PLANTS

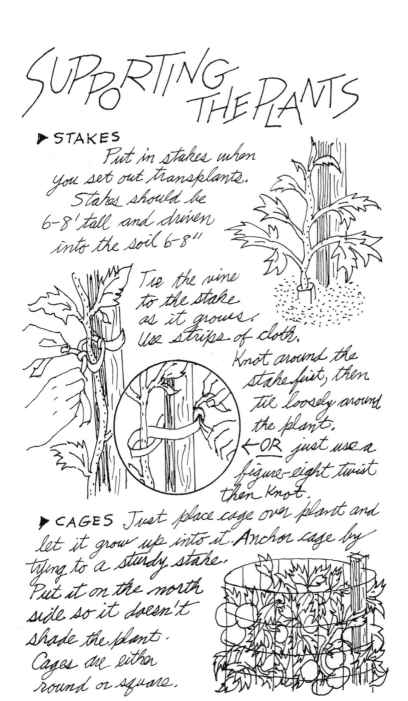

▶ STAKES

Put in stakes when you set out transplants. Stakes should be 6-8' tall and driven into the soil 6-8"

Tie the vine to the stake as it grows. Use strips of cloth.

Knot around the stake first, then tie loosely around the plant.

← OR just use a figure-eight twist then knot.

▶ CAGES Just place cage over plant and let it grow up into it. Anchor cage by tying to a sturdy stake. Put it on the north side so it doesn't shade the plant. Cages are either round or square.

▶ **TRELLIS** Put trellis into position, then push pointed stakes into soil about 8." Set in one transplant at base of each stake

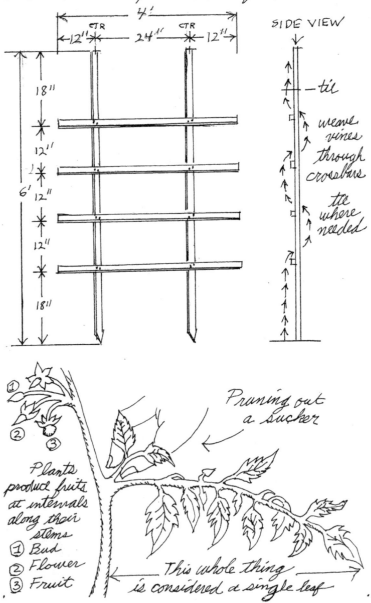

SIDE VIEW

4'

‹12"›‹—CTR— 24" —CTR—›‹— 12" —›

18"

12"

6' 12"

12"

18"

— til

weave vines through crossbars

tie where needed

Pruning out a sucker

① Bud
② Flower
③ Fruit

Plants produce fruits at intervals along their stems

This whole thing is considered a single leaf

own using about 5 feet of 4-foot tall heavy wire fencing. Bend it into a circle and loop the ends into hooks to link together.

Trellising

This is similar to staking but has many places on which you can tie the vines. Trellises can be made in any size, 4 feet wide by 6 feet tall is the best size for the modules. Positioned across the width of the bed it will support two plants.

It is made using 1x2 lumber. Two 6-foot lengths with points cut at their bottom are needed as stakes. Four 4-foot lengths are used for crossbars. The illustration on page 180 shows the construction. Use $1\frac{1}{4}$-inch #6 deck screws to fasten crossbars to stakes, 2 at each stake. The transplants are set in at the stake's base. As the vines grow they are weaved between the crossbars. Tying is done only where it is needed. Do not prune.

Classifications

There are two main types of tomato plants: *determinate* and *indeterminate*. The two classifications refer to the growth habit.

Determinate varieties are mostly small early tomatoes that used to be called bush or dwarf. They do not grow indefinitely at the tip. They develop flower buds between each leaf or between every other leaf. When they reach a certain height, flowers form at the vine tips, then they stop growing and no more fruit forms. They usually produce their fruit during a short span of time. They do not need to be supported.

Indeterminate varieties are mostly the large main-crop tomatoes. They keep growing indefinitely at the tip and do not stop setting fruits until stopped by frost. Flower clusters are always produced on the sides of the stems, usually after every two leafs or after every three leafs. Also side branches, called suckers, will sprout at some of the junctions where the leaf joins the main stem. These develop into additional stems and will produce fruits just like the main stem. Whether to prune or not to prune these suckers is the subject of hot debates.

Most gardeners favor indeterminates because of the larger fruit and greater yield. Because of their extensive growth they are usually staked or supported by other means.

But they don't have to be! If left unsupported they will

require less work and yield more fruits. Drawbacks are that they are more susceptible to diseases, rot, and insect and slug damage. Space required is the biggest disadvantage. One plant can spread for 15 square feet. They have to be spaced 4–5 feet apart and in rows 4–5 feet apart. In the usual backyard this is not practical.

In addition <u>semi-determinates</u> have been developed that have some characteristics of each. Most have the growth habit of determinates but, like the indeterminates, produce fruits over a longer period. There is a wide diversity in this classification, depending on what genes were used in the cross.

Selecting a variety
There are hundreds of varieties available today. But you can narrow the list down a bit if you just visit your local nursery.
They carry only the varieties that are suited to your region.
Also, when looking through seed catalogs, the descriptions will give you some hint as to whether it is bred for commercial or home gardeners. Tomatoes described as excellent shipper or long shelf life are obviously for the commercial growers.

Any variety that has the label "All-America Selections Winner" denotes that that strain has been tested in field trials all over the country and is suitable for growing in any part of the United States. They are usually a good choice.

Then, aside from suitability to your area, obviously you must take into consideration what you are going to use them for, fresh eating, in salads, making sauce, or canning?

Generally you should plant at least two different varieties. If a condition arises that ravages one you will still have a crop from the other. Besides, by choosing strains that mature at different times, the harvest can be stretched. In most areas there will be enough frost-free days to plant an early variety and a main-crop variety that will give an extended harvest. In a short-season area, your choices will be pretty much limited to early tomatoes.

Open-pollinated or hybrid
If you intend to save seed from your crop you need to grow open-pollinated varieties (also called standard). Hybrids are a cross between two genetically distinct parents and their offspring will not be uniform.

Terminology

When looking through seed catalogs or reading the backs of seed packets, it is helpful to understand some of the basic terminology.

Variety names followed by the initials V, F, N, T, and A mean that that variety is resistant or tolerant to the most common tomato problems: verticillium wilt (V), fusarium wilt, race 1 (F), races 1 & 2 (FF), nematodes (N), tobacco mosaic virus (T), and alternaria (A), which is early blight.

Other initials or abbreviations will indicate various aspects of the plant: I, indeterminate; D, determinate; OP, open pollinate; H or HY, hybrid; E, early (up to 65 days); M, midseason (up to 66–79 days); L, late (80+ days). There are many more but most catalogs will have a key to explain what each means.

Pruning

Basically, pruning is the pinching off of the shoots (called suckers) that grow out from the stem right above a leaf branch. (See page 180.) If left to grow, this shoot simply becomes another big stem that will produce fruits the same as all of the others.

Determinate plants should never be pruned. Some semi-determinates grow fairly tall and can be pruned very lightly. Indeterminate varieties are the ones that many choose to prune.

But since pruning takes away stems that will produce fruits and in the long run reduces your yield, why do people prune?

Reasons for pruning

Most commonly, gardeners prune the large indeterminate vines simply to make them easier to manage. It also increases air flow through the plants, lessening the chance of disease.

Some say they prune to get earlier and slightly larger fruits. This is common among those who have a short growing season.

They assert that the stress caused by pruning makes a plant fear it's going to die so it hurries to ripen its fruit. The reason given for bigger fruits is that, since pruning reduces the number of flowers, there is less competition for the nutrition, so each one gets more. Sounds logical, but I have doubts about the claim of bigger fruits.

Before deciding whether to prune or not, just remember that at the end of the season a comparable unpruned plant will have yielded a much bigger overall harvest.

Single-stem pruning
Remove all side branches or suckers leaving only the main stem.
Check plants weekly and remove them right away. Be careful not
to harm any fruit buds or flowers. Also snap off flush with the
main stem any lower leaves that have yellowed.

Multiple-stem pruning
Two or more main stems are allowed to develop. This method will
produce more fruits than the single stem method and also give
more sunscald protection. The only difference between this and
the single stem technique is that one or more suckers near the bottom of the main stem are left to grow into additional main stems,
usually two.

Caged and unsupported plants usually are not pruned
But some gardeners even prune those, randomly pinching out
suckers to control growth—don't ask me why!

To prune or not to prune, that is the question
<u>I am not a fan of pruning.</u> If you decide to prune, be aware that
once started it must be continued every week for the entire growing season. If you stop the plant will become unbalanced.

Storing tomatoes
At season's end, consider anything that can be stored as a bonus.
But, if storing tomatoes at season's end is high on your list of
priorities, you might want to try Burpee's 'Long Keeper.' It is a
variety specifically bred for storage.

Storing Ripe Tomatoes
Ripe tomatoes will keep for several days up to a week in a cool
place. Generally putting ripe tomatoes in the refrigerator is not
recommended as that will diminish their flavor. However, if any of
them are scarred, cracked, or otherwise damaged, put them in the
refrigerator right away to keep from spoiling.

Storing Green Tomatoes
To store green tomatoes spread them out so that they are not
touching each other and cover with paper. Some people like to

wrap them individually in newspaper. Any tomatoes that are stored should be free of cuts or cracks in the skin that will allow decay to set in and ruin the fruit. A long-standing tradition is to put green tomatoes on a sunny window sill to ripen. It's a nice tradition but usually they just turn pink and shrivel up. Light will not ripen them, they do better in darkness.

Trench planting

I have always set in my tomato transplants vertically straight up and down. But there are those who put them in horizontally.

This method requires digging a shallow trench about 2 to 3 inches deep and a little longer than the length of the transplant. All leaves are pinched off except the very top cluster.

The plant is then placed in the trench and the entire stem is covered, leaving just the top leaf cluster sticking out. A little mound of dirt is made under this cluster so that it has a slight upward tilt. Once growth starts it will grow upright.

Proponents say that roots closer to the surface get extra warmth early in the season, causing faster growth. Since more roots form on the buried stem, a stronger plant is the result.

In theory that sounds good, but I conducted a few comparison tests and found those claims to be very questionable. The plants that I set in straight up consistently outperformed the ones put in horizontally. <u>I'll stick with putting them in straight up!</u>

For gardeners living in very short season areas, I can see a certain logic for it. Since tomato plants need as much warmth on the roots as possible, in those areas, it might make a difference.

Also when you have some extremely leggy plants, it makes sense to put those in using the trench planting method.

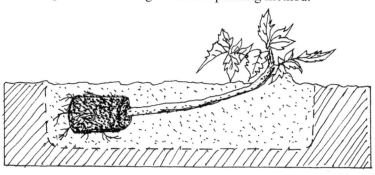

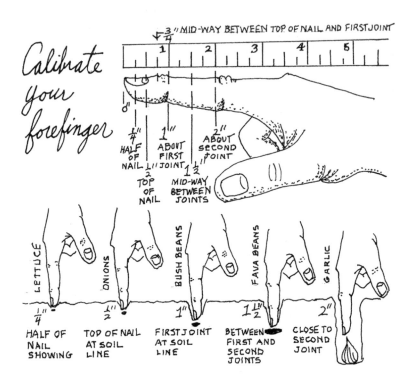

CALIBRATE YOUR FOREFINGER

Place a standard ruler alongside your forefinger and take notice of where the fingernail, first joint, and second joint match up with the ¼-, ½-, ¾-, 1-, 1½-, and 2-inch marks.

The illustration above shows the calibration of my forefinger and some typical plantings.

Depths do not have to be ultra-precise. Notice in the above drawing that the 2-inch mark does not fall exactly on the second joint but slightly below. I gauge that spot by eye. Anything fairly near the joint is considered to be 2 inches.

When small seed sowings are made in flats, push seeds in with tip of finger to ¼- or ½-inch depth. When garden furrows for small seed are made, measure the furrows using your fingertip.

Large seed sowings need to be pushed in deeper. Bush beans call for a planting depth of 1 inch. I simply push seeds in until the first joint of my finger is at the soil line.

For garlic use your calibrated forefinger to make sure that the clove tip is 2 inches below the surface.

186

Index

About the Author

Raymond Nones was born and raised in western Pennsylvania during the Great Depression. Throughout childhood and into adolescence he was taught the skills needed for the growing of vegetables by his father, other neighborhood gardeners, and local farmers.

At age 18, when the nation was involved in World War II, he went into the army, taking part in the liberation of the Philippines as a combat infantryman during the battle to retake Luzon Island.

At war's end he was honorably discharged and attended the Art Institute of Pittsburgh under the G.I. Bill of Rights.

Upon graduation, to begin his professional career in the commercial art field, he relocated to New York City.

After a period of several years he married and bought a home in the borough of Queens, and it was there, in the backyard, that the modular gardening concept was conceived and developed.

During this period Mr. Nones also furthered his education at Queensborough Community College, St. John's University, New York Botanical Gardens, and Queens Botanical Gardens.

A strong believer in promoting home gardening, he has written many articles on the subject of growing vegetables that have appeared as feature articles in several national magazines.

This book is his further attempt to keep the long-standing American tradition of backyard vegetable gardens alive and hopefully to encourage the establishment of more of them.